The Enlightenment of Jesus
Practical Steps to Life Awake

David W. Jones

Valjean Press, Nashville

David Jones is pastor of
Harpeth Presbyterian Church,
Brentwood, Tennessee
and is also the author of:

The Psychology of Jesus:
Practical Help for Living in Relationship

In the Beginning Were the Words:
A Look at the First Chapters of Genesis through Poetry

Contents

Blessed are your eyes, for they see,
and your ears, for they hear.
Jesus (Matthew 13:16)

Encounter One:
Awareness, Awareness, Awareness

I had a dream that I was awake,
and I woke up to find myself asleep.
Stan Laurel

I don't think Jesus is familiar with the proverb, *When the student is ready, the teacher will appear,* because in my life, he just shows up, whether I am ready or not, whether I want him to or not, without invitation or request, fully prayer free, he just shows up.

The first time Jesus appeared to me, I was asleep. Officially Saturday by about three hours, my wife and I, our three children, and both dogs, were all snug in our beds. I was in a deeper than normal sleep when Jesus touched me on the shoulder and whispered, "Wake up."

I stirred. I thought the intrusive hand on my shoulder belonged to my son, Nathan, then four years old. I said, "Nate, go to the bathroom, and then go back to bed. It's still night time. Daddy wants to sleep." Nathan had this habit of coming into our room saying, "Hi," and informing us, "I need to go potty" on his way to the bathroom. He never needed any help, just always thought we'd like to know.

Jesus squeezed my shoulder. He whispered again, "Wake up. I want to talk to you."

I realized this time the voice I was hearing wasn't young like my son's but much older. I opened my eyes to see a shadow standing over me in the dark. Surprisingly, I didn't have a burglar-in-the-house reaction. I wasn't startled. Yet, at the same time, I was startled. I wasn't alarmed, but, at the same time, I was alarmed. Part of me wanted to get up quickly and go with him, and part of me wanted to roll over and see if he would just go so I could sleep on.

Gravity seemed slightly tilted toward following, so I slid out of bed and trailed the shadow. I navigated over a fallen pillow, around the body of our snoring Labrador Retriever, Pooh, through the doorway and into the hall. The figure moved ahead of me without hesitation while I cautiously moved through the house hoping for my toes, knees, and abdomen's sake that there was no discrepancy between my expectations of counter tops, corners and cupboards and where they actually were.

"Who is this?" my mind wondered, "and where are we going?" The shadow led me on with a quiet shepherd-like authority. He walked into the shades of gray of my living room. He sat on the couch shaped blob and, as best as I could tell, motioned for me to sit on the chair next to it. I complied. He said nothing, but looked at me. 'What's he waiting for?' I wondered.

Uncomfortable with the silence, I spoke, "Jesus?"

He said nothing. Just waited. Since the shadow seemed like Jesus, I concluded I should do what dream Jesus said. He told me to wake up, so I tried. If it was a dream, then the shadow would disappear, if not, well, I didn't know. "Okay, dream Jesus," I said, "I'm waking up. What do you have to say to me?" almost begging him to speak and at the same time terrified that he would. Before he could answer, I named my fear, "You're not going to send me off to some foreign land are you? If so, I'd like to request Hawaii over Haiti." I wondered if Jesus found my sarcasm amusing since my family never seemed to.

"No," Jesus laughed. He didn't seem to be laughing at my joke but at me.

"I'm not sending you anywhere," he said. "Before I can send you somewhere you've got to be somewhere."

"Got to be somewhere?" I asked. I heard myself and then wished I could return the words to my mouth. I didn't want Jesus to think I was stupid, but I was confused. I had wanted him to speak, but I had hoped he would make more sense. 'This must be Jesus,' I thought. 'He's speaking in riddles.'

"Right now," he said, "you are only barely here. Only barely present. Only slightly in touch and in tune with the current moment. You move a lot. Your mouth makes sounds as if you are awake, but to those of us who can truly see you, we are not fooled." He laughed again. "Your eyes are still more closed than open. I'm here to help you open your eyes."

With all the energy I could muster, I pried my eyes open. "Okay, Jesus, I'm awake."

"No, you're not," Jesus said. "That's why I'm here."

"I'm awake," I said. "A cup of coffee and I would be more awake, but Jesus, I am awake."

"Awake," Jesus said, "means more than you know. Trust me, you are not awake, but you can be. The first step toward waking up is realizing just how asleep you are. Sleeping people are never aware they are asleep. Only after someone awakens does he or she realize just how asleep they had been. And you, my child, you are sleeping and don't know it."

"More asleep than awake?" I was trying not to disagree with him. After all, even if he was only my dream Jesus, he was still Jesus. I sat up straight. "Look at me, Jesus. Good posture. Open eyes. I'm looking at you. I'm listening. I'm awake."

"Just because your eyes are open doesn't mean you are awake. Just because you look doesn't mean you see. Just because you listen doesn't mean you hear. You are programmed and patterned, living not a human life but instead the life of a machine, a robot, moving constantly but without thought, moving mechanically with little vision, perception, or understanding."

I felt frustrated. "What do you mean, Jesus? A robot? A machine? I'm not a robot! I'm not a machine!" 'Is this some sort of parable?' I wondered. 'Why doesn't Jesus make more sense?' I couldn't recall Jesus ever saying that the kingdom of God was like a robot. I wanted to understand, but my head hurt. I resisted. "Jesus, I'm flesh and blood. I'm not asleep. I'm awake." I couldn't believe I was arguing with Jesus! I realized my mother had always been right. She frequently said I would even argue with God if I got the chance.

"Awake?" Jesus said laughing again.

'If this really is Jesus,' I wondered, 'would he laugh at me? He certainly is not laughing with me.'

"Awake? Not you, my sleeping child," he said. "Pay attention. Consider your life. Your life has come to you as a gift, something to be treasured, experienced, and lived. Yet, you are missing it. You are sleep walking through it."

I liked the image of my life as a gift much more than the accusation of living like a robot. I realized that the shadow before me was talking about more than me rising out of bed to meet with him, that he was talking about me waking to my life, that his judgment of me sleep walking through life wasn't an accusation but an invitation.

"Please," I said, "give me an example of how I sleep walk through life."

"I'll show you in two words," Jesus said.

"Two words?" I asked.

"Two words," he replied. "Strawberry cereal."

"Strawberry cereal?" I asked. "What are you talking about?" I wondered if this was another parable. I was sure I would need some help to understand.

"Strawberry cereal," he responded as if saying the words one more time would trigger my memory.

'Strawberry cereal?' I asked myself finding no help from Jesus. Then I remembered the morning prior. Cayla, my eldest, came into the kitchen. As I had for the previous four months of school mornings, I asked, "What do you want for breakfast?" Each morning prior she had answered, "Strawberry cereal" meaning a Special K cereal with freeze dried strawberries. But on this particular morning, she didn't say the usual, "Strawberry cereal," instead she said, "Honey Nut Cheerios." I even remarked to her, "That's different." "I just wanted something different," she replied. I heard her, but even though part of my brain marked the request for something different, I still went to the cupboard and followed the normal pattern. I grabbed the same strawberry cereal I had each morning before. Not until I placed the bowl in front of her did my mind trigger, 'That's not what she asked for...'

I looked at Jesus. "Strawberry cereal," I admitted. "I guess my mind just shut off."

"Or was asleep," Jesus added. "Do you remember a phone call that morning?"

"I don't remember getting a phone call," I said.

"Not you, Carrie."

"Oh, yes..." My wife, Carrie, had gotten a phone call. Carrie works at our church's preschool. A neighbor had asked if Carrie would drive her daughter to the preschool. The woman's other child was sick. Carrie said that she would. About a half an hour later I got a call from Carrie in her car, "I forgot to go by and get Gracie!" Even though she made a mental note to pick the girl up, she drove off in her normal pattern and forgot her.

"I guess she was asleep, too?" I asked Jesus.

"Now you're getting it. Sleeping people are patterned and don't know it. Sleeping people are like machines with preprogrammed routines. Much of your life you spend asleep, unaware, unawake, just going through the motions, more animated than alive."

Jesus must have sensed my skepticism. "Think about your own driving habits," he challenged me.

"You're suggesting I'm sleep driving? That could be dangerous," but then I answered my own question. I thought about how many times I had left the house, headed for the church where I am pastor, then realized I wasn't going to work but the grocery store. My mind seemed be on auto-pilot. If I didn't focus on the destination, I would consistently turn toward the church.

As if he knew my thoughts, he prodded me further, "Think about the car pool." I immediately knew. Frequently, I fill in for our neighborhood carpool of five girls. The girls like it when I drive because of the game they play. When we get close to our neighborhood, the often ruckus girls go quiet. They say nothing and wait. They have discovered that if they are quiet enough, I fall into the normal routine and turn down our street toward our house forgetting to take the other girls home. Usually, before I get the garage door open, I realize my mistake. I say, "Oh..." and they laugh, more at me than with me. Apparently, to middle school girls, this is extremely funny.

"Do you see your patterns?" Jesus asked.

"I'm starting to," I said.

"Excellent," Jesus said. "This week, just keep looking for your patterns and the patterns of others, in church, in marriage, in family. If you look, you will see patterns that have been shaping and controlling your life and the lives of others, dictating your choices and the choices of others, guiding your actions and the actions of others, all the while unseen."

"Once I see them, do I try and change them?" I asked.

"No," Jesus said. "At first, it is enough for you to simply see the patterns. Don't fight them. Don't resist them. Just see them. The road to your awakening begins with awareness, but not just any awareness. The road to your awakening begins with self awareness. Before you can see the world, you must see yourself. Before you can look into the lives of others, you must take a clear unfettered look into your own life. Self awareness is the doorway to waking up. The first step for your rising out of bed a little while ago was becoming aware that you were being touched. You didn't know who or what was touching you, but you were aware you were being touched." He stood up, "This week, live aware. Specifically, pay attention to your patterns."

"I'll try," I promised.

Jesus was gone. He walked into the shadows of my house and simply dissipated and disappeared.

I sat for a while considering what I had heard. My hands were shaking. My mind was racing but against whom or what I couldn't tell. 'Was the visit a dream? Was I mentally ill? Did I encounter the divine?' I didn't know. Hoping for some comfort, I turned on the lamp by my chair and picked up a Bible from the stack of books next to me. I attempted to open the Bible to the middle in hopes of finding a comforting Psalm, but my hands were shaking so badly, instead of Psalms, I opened to the book of Proverbs. I looked down and read Proverbs 6:9,

> How long will you lie there, O lazybones?
> When will you rise from your sleep?
> A little sleep, a little slumber,
> a little folding of the hands to rest,
> and poverty will come upon you like a robber,
> and want, like an armed warrior.

I closed the Bible and opened it once more, this time to Ephesians 5:14,

> Sleeper, awake!
> Rise from the dead,
> and Christ will shine on you.

In disbelief, I quickly closed my Bible, turned off the light and headed back toward my bed. I stubbed my toe on the coffee table and then bruised my shoulder on our door frame. I stumbled over our dog and then fell into the bed.

"What's wrong?" Carrie asked a third concerned and two thirds disturbed.

"Jesus is bothering me," I said.

"Jesus is bothering you?" she asked.

"Yes," I said, "he won't let me sleep."

Movement:
From life asleep to life awake.

Stepping Stone:
Wake to unconscious patterns.

Unconscious patterns are a clear sign of going through life
asleep. I know about patterns. I'm a pastor.

My church's members are like most others, finding comfort in
familiar practices, arriving at same time, parking in the same spots,
seating themselves in the same pews. Most pray patterned prayers
offering, "Our Father who art..." when we gather and praying "God is
great..." and "Now I lay me..." at home. Those patterns are difficult
to leave behind.

I encourage you to listen to what Jesus said to me, "At first, it is
enough for you to simply see the patterns. Don't fight them. Don't
resist them. Just see them." When I first started to notice my
patterns, I tried to break out of one on a Sunday morning. It did not
go well for me, or my congregation.

After the worship service, I took my position at the front of the
church by the door as usual. As I shook the hands of exiting
parishioners, I greeted and was greeted with, "Have a nice week,"
and, "See you next Sunday."

One of our members, Kathy, shook my hand and said softly,
"Hi, how are you?" without breaking her stride through the door.

I replied, "Fine," but determined to have more than the
patterned response, I resisted Kathy's quick exit. The normal
duration for a handshake was over, but I wasn't finished. She pulled
away, but I held on pulling her back into the doorway. I twisted my
head to make contact with her already-past-me face. She returned to
me. "Kathy," I said pausing for emphasis, "how are you?"

"Fine," she said giving a slight tug of return to her hand.

"No, really Kathy, how ARE you? I want to know." By this time I
just had her fingers, "Are you okay? How was your week? Really, I
want to know."

"It was fine," she said emphatically pulling her hand liberating her fingers. "Fine," she said again. "Really." At this point she was out the door.

I gave her the pastoral I understand nod of my head. 'I think we connected,' I lied to myself. I looked up to see the parishioners now backed up from the exit like a line of women at the bathroom of a college football game, restless and anxious, trying to will the front of the line to move ahead and make way. The path cleared; one by one they all came through. I let them all go, no questions asked.

More and more in my church life, I find that patterns often become traditions. Over time, the founding reasons for the pattern are often forgotten, like the church in this story...

A cat would get in a church sanctuary on Sunday morning, meow loudly, and rub against the legs of parishioners under the pews startling many and disturbing more. So, to keep the cat from disrupting the Sunday Service, each Sunday morning, an elder in the church would catch the cat and tie it up outside. That happened every Sunday for ten years. After ten years, the cat died. The following Sunday, with no cat to tie up, the elder on duty roamed the streets of the town, found another cat, took it to the church, and tied it up outside.

In your life, look at your patterns. Do you see any that have become sacred traditions for reasons since forgotten?

Stepping Stone:
Wake to your family patterns.

"Do you, Roger, take this woman to be your wife?"
"I do."
"And do you, Rebecca, take this man to be your husband?"
"I do."
"By the power vested in me, I now pronounce you man and wife. Let the games begin."

I try and prepare them, those innocent young who come to the church to be married. I try to give them some picture that they have not only chosen each other, they have been chosen by their families, chosen as missionaries, as agents, as representatives. I try to show them how, in their lives up to this point, their families have been preparing them, educating them, training them in the 'right' way to live their family way, their long traditioned, heavily patterned, family way, sending them forth into marriage, to procreate a new family, one with the same values, behaviors, traditions, patterns of the family from whence they came.

I try to prepare individuals who come to me for premarital counseling for the upcoming mêlée. I ask them, "What do you think your marriage will be like?"

I listen to their responses, then I add, "I like to think of marriage as one really long...football game."

Comparing marriage to football is no insult. I come from the South where football is sacred. I would never belittle marriage by saying it is like soccer, bowling, or playing bridge, never. Those images would never work, only football is passionate enough to be compared to marriage. In other sports, players walk onto the field, in football they run onto the field, in high school ripping through some paper, in college (for those who are fortunate enough) they touch the rock and run down the hill onto the field in the middle of the band. In other sports, fans cheer, in football they scream. In other sports, players 'high five', in football they chest, smash shoulder pads, and pat your rear. Football is a passionate sport, and marriage is about passion.

In football, two teams send players onto the field to determine which athletes will win and which will lose, in marriage two families send their representatives forward to see which family will survive and which family will be lost into oblivion with their traditions, patterns, and values lost and forgotten.

Preparing for this struggle for survival, the bride and groom are each set up. Each has been led to believe that their family's patterns are all 'normal,' and anyone who differs is dense, naïve, or stupid because, no matter what the issue, the way their family has always done it is the 'right' way. For the premarital bride and groom in their twenties, as soon as they say, "I do," these 'right' ways of doing things are about to collide like two three hundred and fifty pound linemen at the hiking of the ball. From "I do" forward, if not before, every decision, every action, every goal will be like the line of scrimmage.

Where will the family patterns collide?

In the kitchen. Here the new couple will be faced with the difficult decision of "Where do the cereal bowls go?" Likely, one family's is high, and the others is low. Where will they go now?

In the bathroom. The bathroom is a battleground unmatched in the potential conflicts. Will the toilet paper roll over the top or underneath? Will the acceptable residing position for the lid be up or down? And, of course, what about the toothpaste? Squeeze it from the middle or the end?

But the skirmishes don't stop in the rooms of the house, they are not only locational they are seasonal. The classic battles come home for the holidays.

Thanksgiving. Which family will they spend the noon meal with and which family, if close enough, will have to wait until the nighttime meal, or just dessert if at all?

Christmas. Whose home will they visit first, if at all? How much money will they spend on gifts for his family? for hers?

Then comes for many couples an even bigger challenge – children of their own!

At the wedding, many couples take two candles and light just one often extinguishing their candle as a sign of devotion. The image is Biblical. The Bible is quoted *a man shall leave his father and mother and be joined to his wife, and the two shall become one.* What few prepare them for is the upcoming struggle, the conflict over the unanswered question: the two shall become one, but which one? Two families, two patterns, two ways of doing things, which family's patterns will survive to play another day, in another generation, and which will be lost forever? Let the games begin.

Stepping Stone:
Wake to your family patterns that cross generations.

"Because I said so!" I can still hear my father.

As a determined eight year old, I swore to my father, "I will never say, 'Because I said so' to MY child." Fast forward thirty-five years later, we have three children, Cayla, Abbie, and Nathan. Each, at one time or another, has heard me say, "Because I said so." Each has also heard me lecture them on the evils of not eating their supper while there are so many starving children in India, another thing I swore I would never say to my child. The patterns we learn as children resurface when we become parents, no matter how dormant we thought them to be.

What I have found even more amazing is just how unquestioned our family patterns can become. Sensible or not, we assume our way of doing things is the 'right' way, like in this story...

Every time Mary cooked a roast, she cut off a small slice on each end. A neighbor, over sharing a cup of coffee, watched her semi-consciously cut off the ends. "Why do you do that?" asked the neighbor.

Mary thought about it. She didn't know. "I guess it's because that's the way my mother always cooked a roast." She was a little embarrassed that she had no other reason, so she called her mother. Her mother told her that she, like her daughter, simply cut the ends off the roast because she had seen her mother do the same. Mary called grandma. Her grandmother explained that she had always cut the ends off the roast because the pot she used was a small pot, too small for a normal roast. She cut the ends off to make the roast fit in the pot. Mary realized that two generations later she kept the same pattern of her grandmother even though they no longer owned the small pot nor needed to cut the ends off the roast.

We observe and imitate. The patterned way is assumed the preferable way, the right way, the best way, and why wouldn't we pass on the best way to the next generation?

What family patterns do you have which have crossed generations? Do you know why you do the things you do? Are there any patterns in your family or in your life which have been held with football-like religious fervor?

Stepping Stone:
Commit to changing patterns that keep you asleep.

Are you ever like the Bear in the following story?

Borshka, the dancing circus bear, lived in a cage. The cage was so small that all he could do was take three steps in one direction, turn around, and take three steps back. When it was time for him to perform, his trainer would put a large chain around his neck and lead him out to the circus crowd. When his performance was over, his trainer would lead him back to his cage. In his cage, he could take three steps forward, turn around, and three steps back.

The circus shut down. There were no shows, only the cage for Borshka. After some time, a man came to see the circus and felt sorry for the poor bear who once was a star but now lived in a cage where he could only take three steps forward and three steps back. The man bought Borshka from the circus, took him cage and all on a long train ride to the edge of the mountains. He had the conductor stop the train. They took Borshka, cage and all off the train. The man opened up the cage door, Borshka stepped out. He saw the beautiful mountains with all the trees. In the distance he could see a water fall with crisp clear water and probably a stream with lots of fish. Then Borshka, in the middle of the wilderness, did what he always did - took three steps forward, and three steps back. Three steps forward, and three steps back.

This week, in some way, try four steps forward, and four steps back... and pay attention to your commitment to your patterns.

The Enlightenment of Jesus:

Jesus wasn't fond of patterned religion or patterned relationships. He showed his distaste for unquestioned patterns and his love for awakening minds in his lifting up the lifestyle of Mary over Martha.

Luke 10: *Now as they went on their way, (Jesus) entered a certain village, where a woman named Martha welcomed him into her home. She had a sister named Mary, who sat at the Lord's feet and listened to what he was saying. But Martha was distracted by her many tasks; so she came to him and asked, 'Lord, do you not care that my sister has left me to do all the work by myself? Tell her then to help me.' But the Lord answered her, 'Martha, Martha, you are worried and distracted by many things; there is need of only one thing. Mary has chosen the better part, which will not be taken away from her.'*

Two women, Mary and Martha, one busy, one sitting at the feet of Jesus, Martha locked in her dutiful pattern, Mary doing her best to see and to hear. Jesus affirmed Mary's attempts to see and hear and discouraged Martha's patterned duty. Jesus encouraged the wakening choice of Mary to the going through the motions of Martha.

In similar fashion, Buddha encouraged mindful attention over mindless duty. In an ancient story...

The Buddha was asked, "Sir, what do you and your monks practice?"
He replied, "We sit, we walk, and we eat."
"But sir, everyone sits, walks and eats."
"Ahh," the Buddha replied, "but when we sit, we know that we are
sitting. When we walk, we know that we are walking and when we eat, we
know that we are eating."

Jesus wants similar awareness from his disciples. He says to his followers in Matthew 13: [16]*blessed are your eyes, for they see, and your ears, for they hear.* Seeing, hearing, understanding... so simple, yet often so difficult, at least for the habitually asleep.

How can you be more like Mary than Martha this week? How can you sit when you are sitting, walk when you are walking, and eat when you are eating?

Reflection:

Read the following quotes. How does each relate to the steps toward enlightenment described in this chapter?

Instead of asking "Why are we here?"
We should ask, "Are we here?"
Leonard Nimoy

People usually consider walking on water
or in thin air a miracle.
But I think the real miracle is not
to walk either on water or in thin air,
but to walk on earth.
Thich Nhat Hanh

Open my eyes that I may see
Glimpses of truth Thou hast for me;
Place in my hands the wonderful key
That shall unclasp and set me free.
Clara H. Scott

The man who is aware of himself is henceforward independent;
and he is never bored, and life is only too short,
and he is steeped through and through
with a profound yet temperate happiness.
Virginia Woolf

The third gate of dreaming is reached
when you find yourself in a dream,
staring at someone else who is asleep.
And that someone else turns out to be you
Carlos Castaneda

If we could see the miracle of a single flower clearly,
our whole life would change.
Buddha

Now what?

To help people find enlightenment, Buddha spent little time teaching people how to think. He showed little concern over what people thought. Instead, his teachings were programs for action. Jesus was similar. In the gospels, the word *do* shows up 487 times but the word *believe* is used only 88. Buddha and Jesus both emphasized action.

Accordingly, at the end of each chapter is a section entitled, *Now what?* In this section will be exercises giving some practical ways for you to walk across the stepping stones and take action toward your own enlightenment.

To awaken to your patterns, try the following: Use the chart on the next page to journal your patterns this week. Fill in the columns. Under *Patterns* write things you do each specific day. For example, if every Sunday night you call your mother, child, or another relative, write it by *Sunday*. For things you do everyday, or most days, write them beside *Daily*. For example, if every morning you have a cup of coffee and watch the morning news, include this in your *Daily* list.

At the end of the week go back and reflect. Circle every pattern which if you cut out of your routine would create tension for you. Put a line through every pattern you think is keeping you from waking to your life. Look closely at the patterns you put a line through.

Next, write what you'll do differently this week to awaken from those patterns which might be keeping you asleep.

Day	Patterns
Daily	
Sunday	
Monday	
Tuesday	
Wednesday	
Thursday	
Friday	
Saturday	

Encounter Two:
Full Minds Create Chaos

All experience is preceded by mind,
Led by mind,
Made by mind,
The Dhammapada (translated by Gil Fronsdale)

I generally like rules. Rules are helpful. I usually don't break
them without some forethought. So when I tell you I broke a law, I
want you to know that I take rules very seriously, at least most of
them.

Riding my bicycle on the ample shoulder of a four lane road
near our home, ideal weather, wind resistance low, my anticipation
high, after a day saturated with the desire to be outside, I was finally
free. Once finally mounting my metal steed, I strode forward and
away from work and home with the zeal of a man recently given a
governor's pardon. Pedaling faster than my body had hoped,
celebrating the limitless though crowded road in front of me, I sailed
through the first red light and onto the second, both T intersections,
road free on my side, shoulder abounding. With no concern of
anyone crossing my path, I came alongside a rush hour line of
predominantly SUV's waiting at the second light. Due to the size of
the SUV's stopped alongside me, I couldn't see the green lighted
traffic, but since they were only turning right and left I gave them
little thought, until I sailed to the intersection and saw the car.

My assumption that no one would pass in front of me at this
particular intersection needed a qualifier: no one would cross in
front of me, unless they were going into a driveway of a house I had
never noticed before. The car, which seemed to appear out of
nowhere, was heading into the driveway. SUV's to the left of me,
trees to the right, and this new manifested obstacle directly in front, I
squeezed my brakes. I quickly awoke to a maintenance issue I had let
lapse. I had neglected to replace my rear brakes which I then
understood to be quite worn. The reason I was aware of the deficient
brake pads on the bike's rear was that as I grasped both brake
handles, my front tire held while my rear tire kept moving, propelling

the back end of my bike skyward. I have ridden enough to know that a healthy stop requires a deceleration of both front and rear tires. Just shy of ninety degrees, rather than having my rear tire pass my front, I let go of both brakes. That's when I introduced myself to the passenger of the car in front of me.

The woman was obviously quite startled. She didn't see me coming. She was looking straight ahead. I thought, "Boy, will she be surprised." She was. I smashed into the passenger side of the car, startling both passenger and driver alike. The passenger turned to look at me, my face smushed against the glass of her window. Instinctively, both her hands went up protecting herself from my body which had become a fleshy projectile momentarily halted in time and space by her window. I imagine she was even more surprised by my disappearance, for as I had so quickly appeared inches from her face, gravity took over and I vanished from sight, falling to the ground.

I fared better than the car ($1700 in damage). I healed on my own.

A couple of weeks later, I took my bike to the shop. No problem to the frame. I had gears tuned up, the chain and brakes replaced.

In thinking about my next bicycle ride, I realized that my attitude about cars had changed. Whereas I once saw a busy street as an opportunity for fun, I then, post accident, envisioned a crowded road as a frightful place where cars appeared out of nowhere. For my own safety and wellbeing, I sought a trek free from materializing automobiles, so I went to ride in Warner Park. The roads in Warner Park present a challenging ride full of hills and curves with canopies of trees stretching out over the road, but most importantly, Warner Park is relatively car free.

As I started my ride, my accident still forefront in my thoughts, I was only semi-sure I wouldn't encounter a car here, hadn't I been sure before? I also wondered about the barrier-free sides of the road, some of which had hills that dropped thirty feet or more. "What might happen here?" I asked and my anxious mind answered with visions of me skidding or sliding down embankment after embankment into tree after tree.

As I rode along, I noticed some differences in my bike since the tune up, particularly that my brakes were tight compared to the nonexistent ones I had before. I decided that, to be safe, I should test them out to see just how tight, after all, I didn't want to have another accident. I gave them a good squeeze. At that point, and only then, did I realize the sharpness of the curve I was on and the dampness of the road. Other roads were dry, but because the park was so well shaded by hill and tree, the road was wet, and mossy, this I discovered because when I squeezed my rear brakes, my back tire slid out from under me, and bike and I went sliding along the pavement. Pants and shirt absorbed some of the slide, until they shredded. Then it was simply skin meeting asphalt.

I limply peddled back toward the car. I passed a walker who, upon viewing my shredded clothes and raw skin uttered a shocked, "Oh!" After great effort, I returned to my car, loaded the bike, and left the park. It was then that Jesus appeared in the passenger seat beside me.

"Full minds create chaos," he said.

I was in no mood for education. "Have you ever heard the saying, *When the student is ready, the teacher will appear?*" I asked.

"What do you think?" he replied.

"I think I'll live," I said. "'I think I'll live' is the answer to the question, 'Are you okay?'"

"I know you'll live," he said. "I'm Jesus."

"Right," I said.

"And because I'm Jesus," he continued, "I knew you might miss this prime learning opportunity."

"Learning opportunity?" I asked.

"Yes," he said. "Every thing that happens to you, every experience you have, is a learning opportunity. You can learn so much from life if you simply pay attention."

I said nothing.

Jesus sighed. He continued, "It saddens me to think just how many opportunities are missed because people, because you, don't pay attention. Full minds don't learn much."

"No?" I asked as if interested in the conversation. My leg and hip were hurting, probably due to the lack of flesh where my skin once was. I tried to ignore the throbbing enough to drive and not have Jesus telling me later how painful legs create car crashes. He talked some more. I'm sure it was wise, but I didn't hear any of it. I tuned back in once I settled on the main road out of the park.

"Full minds don't learn much," Jesus continued. "However, they do create much."

"Full minds create?" I asked.

"Yes," he said. "Full minds create chaos. Weren't you paying attention?"

"I..." I had nothing, so I just hushed and looked at the road.

"Your full mind," Jesus said, "created your accident."

My curiosity distracted me from my leg. "What?" I asked. "I thought gravity created my accident."

"Gravity affected your destination when you fell, but your fall started in your mind. Your fear imagined an accident. Your body created the accident in response to your mind. Your mind, full of fear and thoughts of pain, created the chaos of your fall and the pain you're now experiencing."

"Full minds create chaos," I said repeating him.

"Right," he said, "your mind was full of accident, so, chaotically, you created what you were afraid of, another accident. See?" he asked. "A learning opportunity."

"Right," I said.

He looked over to my hip. "That road rash will serve as a reminder, serve as a book mark in the book of you."

"The book of me?" I asked.

"Yes," Jesus said. "Think of your life as a book. Read your life like you read a book for every experience is..."

"I know," I said. "An opportunity to learn. That's just great. I do just love learning opportunities." It was almost as if my leg itself were talking through me to Jesus. "Out of curiosity, wise teacher, couldn't you have appeared a little sooner? Maybe, as I was starting the ride? Don't you think that lesson would have been a little timelier?"

"What would you have wanted me to say?" Jesus asked.

"How about 'Be careful?'" I said.

"That wouldn't have helped," Jesus replied. "You were already so full of care and concern that you created an accident. Maybe I should have said, 'Your brakes are very tight so don't squeeze them hard unless you want to slide down the road on your ass.'"

'Could this really be Jesus?' I asked myself. 'Would Jesus use language my mother would find offensive?'

"You should hear the language your mother uses in her own mind," Jesus said.

"Full minds create chaos," I repeated. "So my mind was full of fear."

"Fear," he said, "and images."

"Images?" I asked.

"Images," he continued. "In this case, images of *what might happen*. Those are fabricated in response to your fears. In this instance, your mind was so full of *what might happen* that you missed paying attention, and in fact, facilitated what you were afraid of, all because your mind was full. Empty minds pay attention. Full minds create chaos, and pain. Lots of pain."

"I understand what you mean about pain," I said as my leg was beginning to throb.

We rode along together for a while.

"Say, you're known as 'the great physician,'" I said. "So, what do you think, O' surgeon divine, what should I do to treat my hip and leg."

Jesus looked over at my wound, "If it were me," he said, "I'd go see a doctor."

And he was gone.

Movement:
From a full mind to a clear mind.

Stepping Stone:
See your fears and the power they have over you.

A mind can be full of many dangerous things: anger, desire, frustration, irritation, confusion, longing... but most of all, fear.

Fear is itself frightening, because fear can create realities. Of my two bicycle accidents, the greater injury came from the second, the one caused by my own fear. Fear can injure; fear can maim; fear can kill.

Psychologist Eric Blumenthal reported that in India people frequently die after being bitten by nonpoisonous snakes. Many snakes in India are poisonous, and many people are bitten and die. But sometimes, after the person dies, the snake that bit him is found, in the home for example, and found not to be poisonous. The expectation that the snake was poisonous can be so strong, the expectation alone can kill.

To show the danger of fear, Blumenthal also cited a train depot worker at his job loading the refrigerator car of a train. After the car was loaded, while one employee was still inside, another shut and locked the door. The man inside yelled and pounded on the door, but no one heard him, and all went home. Besides forgetting to check the inside of the car to make sure everyone was out, the errant employee also forgot to turn on the refrigeration unit. The man trapped inside was certain the unit had been turned on, certain it would be another town and twenty-four hours before anyone opened the door, certain he wouldn't survive. His certainty became a self fulfilling prophecy. The next day they opened the car. The temperature inside was quite normal, but the man's lifeless body showed some signs of hypothermia.

Your parents warned you about lightening, about snakes, and about the opposite sex – but did they warn you how dangerous your fears could be all by themselves?

Stepping Stone:
See where your fears reside – all your fears reside inside!

Here are two similar stories about the home of fear and how dangerous it can be when we look outside ourselves for the source of our fears.

There once was a man who had two great fears, shadows and footsteps. One day, he looked over his shoulder to see his shadow. Frightened, he started running. As he ran, he heard footsteps and became more afraid. The faster he ran the more footsteps he heard. He finally died of exhaustion.

Once a monk, while meditating in his room, saw a large spider descending in front of him. Each day, as he began to meditate, the spider would descend and he would run away. After several days of interrupted meditation, he went to the kitchen and returned with a butcher knife. On the way back to his room, he saw his teacher in the hallway.

"Where are you going?" the teacher asked.

"I'm going back to my room to meditate," he said.

"What are you doing with the knife?" the teacher asked.

"Everyday, as I begin my meditation, a spider drops from the ceiling and interrupts me. Today, I'm going to kill the giant spider with this knife."

"Fine," said the teacher. "Before you stab the spider, get some paint and mark it with an X."

The student did as his teacher instructed. He started to meditate, the large spider descended in front of him. He painted it with an X. As soon as he painted the X, the spider disappeared.

Puzzled, he got up and walked around his room. He looked in the mirror to see a large X painted on his head.

We seldom deal with our fears simply because we look elsewhere for their root. However, fears are not external but an internal response to external circumstances. Our fears cause the most harm to us when we look outside ourselves instead of looking within.

Stepping Stone:
*See how full minds, especially fearful minds,
can create chaos for others.*

As 'good' parents, we wanted to keep our children safe. So, we warned each child early on, pointing out potential, life and wellbeing threatening dangers. Perhaps, in reflection, we may have been a little overly cautious. Here was one of the first signs.

Our second child, Abbie, had heard us quite a few times pointing out dangers for her. We didn't think we had overdone it, until, when asked, "What is your name?" Her reply was "Abbie No."

"Abbie No?" we wondered.

Then we realized, "Abbie, no," was a phrase she had so often heard that she deduced that "No" was her last name.

She's going near the stairs! "Abbie, no!"

She's about to grab the iron! "Abbie, no!"

She's sticking the fork in her ear! "Abbie, no!"

Serpents unaware are dangerous, but nothing compared to unseen anxieties and fears inside our minds, and the minds of our parents.

Did your parents' anxiety about you create a mind prone to seeing the world as a terrifying and frightful place?

Stepping Stone:
Use your mind instead of letting it using you.

Eckhardt Tolle said, "For many of us, our minds use us, rather than us using our minds."

We cannot always choose events, but we can choose how we respond to them. For example, my daughter Abbie, second grader at the time, came home from school. After having a snack, playing with her brother, and upon turning toward homework, I heard her in her room crying loudly.

I went to see what was wrong. She had forgotten her homework assignment sheet.

In her class, the teacher had a homework sheet each student was responsible for picking up from her desk. Abbie continually got sidetracked and forgot her homework assignment. A week prior, in order to solve this problem, she and I tied a long red string to the zipper of her back pack. The idea was that each afternoon, when she was packing up to come home, she would see the red string and remember to get her homework assignment before she closed her book bag. Our plan worked four out of five days. This was the fifth day.

She was lying upon the floor, crying, her arm over her eyes. I stretched out on the floor beside her. She looked over at me, half uncovering her eyes. "I just want to see what you see," I said looking up at the ceiling fan in her room.

She half laughed and then kept crying.

"Abbie?" I asked. "Can I tell you a story?"

She nodded.

"When I was in high school, I was on my way to school. I was late for school, but had to stop for gas or I wouldn't make it at all. In a hurry, I decided I wouldn't take my keys from the car. However, because I always locked the car door, automatically I locked the door when I got out with the keys inside. My mother had to come and unlock my car. Already late for school, I felt very dumb. Feeling dumb was okay, because I was determined not to lock my keys in the car again. I used feeling bad to change my behavior and do something different. Do you understand?"

She nodded.

"Now, I'm looking at you on the floor thinking you are in a similar predicament. Are you feeling frustrated, like you did something dumb?"

She nodded.

"Ask yourself; will being upset about forgetting your homework sheet help you remember not to forget it next time?"

"No," she replied.

"Will crying about forgetting your homework get a homework sheet to magically appear?"

"No," she replied.

"Will it somehow get your homework done for you?"

"No," she replied.

"Well," I said, "to me it doesn't seem like a good use of your energy. You can cry if you want to, but if it won't get your homework done or bring you a homework sheet, then why waste the energy? Why don't we go play something? How about a game?"

"Okay," she said. And off she went.

Abbie separated what she could change and what she couldn't. She examined how her remorse for forgetting her assignment and anxiety about the next day at school might serve her. When they offered her nothing, she abandoned them for a better choice – joy!

How can you choose your responses to your emotions rather than letting them control you?

Stepping Stone:
Distinguish between what you can choose and what you can't.

Consider the following story. What is its message about enjoying life?

There once was a man who was being chased by a tiger. He was looking back to see if the tiger was gaining on him and ran off the edge of a cliff. He grabbed a vine sticking out of the cliff and held on tight. He looked up to see the tiger pawing down at him from atop the cliff. Below he saw a long fall and another tiger awaiting him at the bottom. He also noticed the vine he was holding onto was pulling from the cliff. On the vine was a strawberry. He took the strawberry and ate it. The taste was wonderfully sweet.

My first reaction to this parable years ago was 'How depressing! Tiger above, tiger below, breaking vine! Throw the strawberry at the tiger below. Maybe he hates fruit!' Yet, the parable offers a secret to a happy life. To find the secret, we must ask a question about the man; with the vine breaking, tiger above and tiger below, how could he possibly enjoy a strawberry?

To understand the parable, Niebuhr's prayer helps. *God grant me the serenity to accept the things I cannot change; the courage to change the things I can; and the wisdom to know the difference.* Look at the story with Niebuhr's categories:

Things the man on the vine cannot change: having fallen off the cliff, tiger above, tiger below, failing vine.

Things he can change: very little. There is nothing he can do at that moment to chase the tigers away or strengthen the vine.

What he can do: enjoy the strawberry. Worrying about the vine, fear of what the tigers will do, anxiety about falling wouldn't serve him well at all. What would serve him well? Using what little energy he has to enjoy the strawberry.

The secret to a happy life is a wise use of energy. We cannot enjoy any present moments when we focus our limited energies on what we have no control over. However, if we can distinguish the changeable from the unchangeable, joy is ours.

What strawberries have you been missing because you've been using what little energy you have on anxiety?

The Enlightenment of Jesus:

There is a lot of material on fear in the life and teachings of Jesus. For Jesus, doubt doesn't seem to have been the opposite of faith. Fear is. In the following passage from the Sermon on the Mount, Jesus shows a clear understanding of how fear can cloud our minds but faith can open a way to joy. Jesus said...

Matthew 6: [25] *"Therefore I tell you, do not worry about your life, what you will eat or what you will drink, or about your body, what you will wear. Is not life more than food, and the body more than clothing?* [26] *Look at the birds of the air; they neither sow nor reap nor gather into barns, and yet your heavenly Father feeds them. Are you not of more value than they?* [27] *And can any of you by worrying add a single hour to your span of life?* [28] *And why do you worry about clothing? Consider the lilies of the field, how they grow; they neither toil nor spin,* [29] *yet I tell you, even Solomon in all his glory was not clothed like one of these.* [30] *But if God so clothes the grass of the field, which is alive today and tomorrow is thrown into the oven, will he not much more clothe you—you of little faith?* [31] *Therefore do not worry, saying, 'What will we eat?' or 'What will we drink?' or 'What will we wear?'...* [34] *"So do not worry about tomorrow, for tomorrow will bring worries of its own. Today's trouble is enough for today.*

How can you let go of tomorrow's troubles and live today?

Reflection:

Read the following quotes. How does each relate to the steps toward enlightenment described in this chapter?

All experience is preceded by mind,
Led by mind,
Made by mind,
Speak or act with a corrupted mind,
and suffering follows
as the wagon wheel follows the hoof of an ox.

All experience is preceded by mind,
Led by mind,
Made by mind,
Speak or act with a peaceful mind,
and happiness follows
like a never departed shadow.
The Dhammapada (translated by Gil Fronsdale)

If the eye is unobstructed, it results in sight;
if the ear is unobstructed, the result is hearing;
if the nose is unobstructed, the result is a sense of smell;
if the mouth is unobstructed, the result is a sense of taste;
if the mind is unobstructed, the result is wisdom.
Chuang Tzu

The outward freedom that we shall attain will only be in exact proportion to
the inward freedom to which we may have grown at a given moment. And if
this is a correct view of freedom, our chief energy must be concentrated on
achieving reform from within.
Gandhi

Get a grip on your mind.
Buddha

Now what?

Use the space below to answer the following question:
What am I afraid of?

Look again at the above list you created.

Put an asterisk by each fear that you think might be a self fulfilling prophecy. For example, on my bike ride, I was afraid of falling and my fear created my fall.

What practical steps will you take to free yourself from your fears?

What energies have you wasted worrying? Is there a better way to spend your life?

What will you do differently this week?

Encounter Three:
Image of Self

What lies behind us and what lies before us
are tiny matters compared to what lies within us.
Ralph Waldo Emerson

The next time I saw Jesus, I was sitting at my computer. The rest of the house was asleep. I had gotten out of bed, gone to the computer. I googled intelligence tests and started answering questions.

1. *The day before yesterday is four days after Saturday. What day is it today?*
      A. *Monday*
      B. *Tuesday*
      C. *Wednesday*
      D. *Thursday*
      E. *Friday*

Four days after Saturday is Wednesday. The day before yesterday is two days back from today. The answer is *Friday*.

2. *Which number should come next in the series: 6, 7, 9, 12, 16...*
      A. *8*
      B. *11*
      C. *24*
      D. *21*
      E. *27*

The number added is increasing by 1 each time, so the answer is 21.

3. *Book is to page as library is to...*
      A. *building*
      B. *government*
      C. *sidewalk*
      D. *book*

Books hold pages. Libraries hold books. The answer is *book*.

4. Which two words are closest in meaning: scruffy, synthetic, artistic, different, pseudo, figurative?

That's when Jesus appeared. Standing behind me, he placed his hand on my shoulder. I startled.

"Synthetic and pseudo," he said.

"What?" I asked.

"Synthetic and pseudo is the answer," he said. "You're taking a test, and I want to help. Synthetic and pseudo is the answer, both are fake, artificial, inauthentic. The answers to the next three questions are: parakeet, oligarchy and the letter K."

"Wait a minute," I said, "I'm taking the test."

"Yes you are, and it's a good thing I'm here. You would have missed two out of the next three. You have no idea what an oligarchy is and on the one after, you have to give a number value on the letters based on their place in the alphabet. You wouldn't have thought of that. You would have missed it and spent too much time on it."

"But, I was taking the test."

"Yes," he said. "You wanted to get as many of the answers right as you could. I was helping."

"No," I said, "you weren't helping. I was taking the test. I wanted to get the answers right. If you give me the answers, then the score means nothing."

"Oh," Jesus said, "you think the score will mean something? You think you can learn something about yourself from this test? From the score?"

"Yes," I said.

"Are you really here to learn something about yourself?" Jesus asked.

I didn't answer. I was confident that was what I wanted, until Jesus questioned me. "I thought so. Isn't that why I'm here? Isn't my motivation for taking an I.Q. test to learn something about myself? You told me to pay attention to myself, to learn more. Can't I learn more about myself from an accurate score, of my I.Q.?"

"Oh," said Jesus, "you're trying to learn about yourself from intelligence questions. Then here's a question to test your intelligence, 'Why did the chicken cross the road?'"

"To get to the other side," I said.

"Correct," Jesus said. "Ten points!"

"Funny," I said.

"Have you ever wondered what was on the other side that the chicken is risking all to get there?" he asked.

"No, but don't you know? After all, you're Jesus, not me."

"Correct! Ten more points. Even though you don't know exactly what he was after, you do know it was something that interested him, pulled him, motivated him. You know the chicken crossed the road because he was motivated. He had a goal. So, once again, why did the chicken cross the road?"

"Because he was motivated. He had a goal," I said.

"Correct! Ten more points, plus five for paying attention. Now, the more personal question, why did you, the sleepy man, get out of bed and cross the house to take this test?"

"Because I was motivated," I said.

"Yes," Jesus said, "but by what? What was your goal? Were you awake enough to see it, or just sleep walking? If you want to learn something about yourself, forget the test questions and answer this one, 'What was your motivation in taking the test? What was your goal? What pulled you from the bed across the house?'"

I thought for a moment. "I wanted to learn more about myself, more about who I am."

"No," he said. "Incorrect! That's not what got you out of bed. There was a deeper driver. Look closer. Forget the test. Pay attention to yourself. What was your motivation? You didn't come out here to learn about yourself. You weren't trying to learn anything new. You were trying to justify something old, something in you. You started taking this test to validate what you already think about yourself."

"What I already think? But I don't know how I would score," I said.

"No, you don't. The score is not what you were after. You weren't taking this test to see if you are smart or not, you already think you are smart. You wanted the I.Q. score to justify it, to compare you to others so that you could say to yourself, 'I was right! I am smart!'"

"So, I started this test not to find out about myself, but to justify what I already think?"

"Yes," Jesus said, "you started this test for the same reason you got on the bathroom scale this morning."

"I'm taking this test because I think I'm overweight?" I asked.

"No, you think you're overweight and that's why you got on the scale. You knew you had put on a few pounds. You were beating yourself up about it. You got on the scale to prove your image of yourself was right. You see yourself as overweight and used the scale to prove it. Tonight, you were feeling bad about yourself, frustrated by your scale score this morning, accusing yourself of a lack of discipline, a lack of control. So, in order to feel better, you decided to take a test you thought you could do well at, the I.Q. test. You wanted to feel better. You thought this test would do it for you."

"That was my motivation? To feel better?" I asked.

"Yes, you wanted to feel better."

"I wanted to feel better by proving I'm smart?" I asked.

"Yes," he said, "smart is one of the images you have of yourself."

"It is?" I asked.

"Yes, and in your mind, smart people have high I.Q. scores. Therefore, to prove you're smart, you sought a high I.Q. score. If you had scored low, you probably would have said, 'That's just a free internet test. You get what you pay for,' and belittled the test. The image in your mind hungered for justification. You were trying to feed it."

"Image?" I asked. "You keep using that word. What do you mean?"

"Your mind thinks in images. Images to your mind are what words are to your vocabulary. Images seen can be helpful. When you leave your house, and you want to go to the church, you know how to get there because in your mind is an image of the road. When you go to the grocery store to buy milk, you know what milk looks like because in your mind is an image of a gallon of milk. You even have an image of the grocery store already in your mind that helps you navigate through the store to the dairy section."

"Images are maps," I said.

"Some are," Jesus replied, "but most are not. Those are the dangerous ones, those which are unseen, unchallenged, unquestioned. They are images you have of God, the world, life, other people, and yourself. You've heard the term 'self image'?"

"I have."

"You were taking this I.Q. test to justify a self image you already have in your head. You like to image yourself as smart, and you're hoping that taking this test will justify that image, confirm for you what you already think. There is more to be learned about yourself from examining why you want to take this test and what you'll hope it will prove for you than in answering all the questions on the test itself. You can learn more about yourself by examining your motives to take this test than you can from the test."

He was quiet for a moment, he let what he said sink in, and then he said, "Let me sit in front of the computer."

I moved out of the way. Jesus sat down. Jesus googled *quotes*. After a few clicks, Jesus said, "Read this."

Look into the depths of your own soul and learn to know yourself, then you will understand... Freud

He clicked again. *The more faithfully you listen to the voice within you, the better you hear what is sounding outside of you.* Dag Hammarskjold

And again. *Each man's life represents a road toward himself.* Hermann Hesse

And again. *Everything in your life is there as a vehicle for your transformation. Use it!* Ram Dass

"Today," Jesus continued, "you have already been given another learning opportunity. Your teacher is waiting for you, ready to appear, the question is, when she presents herself, will you be ready? Will you see her for what she is, an opportunity? A gift?"

"I guess," I said.

"Good enough," Jesus said. "Let the learning begin."

He clicked again. "Two more quotes. First..."

Let us not look back in anger or forward in fear, but around in awareness. James Thurber

"And..." *Through our senses the world appears. Through our reactions we create delusions. Without reactions the world becomes clear.* Buddha

We were quiet. Jesus stood up. He pointed for me to sit down. I did.

"Read those last two quotes again," he instructed. "Out loud."

I read them again. *Let us not look back in anger or forward in fear, but around in awareness.* And *Through our senses the world appears. Through our reactions we create delusions. Without reactions the world becomes clear.*

"Good enough," he said. "Now, pay attention to each experience. Each experience, each encounter is an opportunity to learn about yourself, to dive into the book that is you. See all your self images and their external manifestations. Use your reactions as a door to your self."

"Door to myself?" I asked.

"Yes," Jesus said. "When you feel a reaction to a situation or experience, look inward. Emotions, especially negative ones, are the doorway to your self. Every negative emotion should point you back to self, not to the outside world, especially when you feel angry or insulted. Remember, whenever you feel insulted, there is an image of self, a self image, involved. Insults to an image will likely stir either a fight or flight reaction from you because you feel offended. However, without the image, there is no offense, no insult, no perceived transgression. Instead of anger, frustration, resentment or retaliation...learn, see, understand, grow. The more you see, the more awake you will become."

Sitting at the computer, I felt as a pilot about to take off down the runway to solo. I wanted gauges to check. I wanted information of the weather ahead. Yet, all I looked at was the screen. *Through our reactions we create delusions. Without reactions the world becomes clear.*

"When will my teacher get here?" I asked.

Jesus laughed. "Check your email."

He was gone.

I was alone.

As instructed, I opened my email folder. I expected several, but to my surprise, there was only one email in my Inbox. A member of the Session (our church's leadership board) had sent me a message. The subject of the email was *Last Night's Meeting*. The night before, the Session had met for its monthly meeting. The only unique item on the agenda had been a decision to cut down a tree in the front yard which blocked our sign from the road.

In the email, the elder accused me of *railroading my agenda through the Session*, of *micro managing* and *not allowing anyone's opinions to be shared*. My character was indicted as I was described as a *shallow, threatened, child with no business in ministry*. My values were also brought to trial with the accusation that I am *superficial and have little appreciation for what is truly important*.

I was stunned. I thought the meeting had gone fine. The decision to cut down the tree had little discussion. There seemed to be a little tension in the air after the meeting ended. People left quickly, a little quicker than normal. Other than that, I didn't notice anything different.

I couldn't believe Jesus had sent me to this email. Was Jesus pointing out to me all my faults? Was this person serving as a messenger from God to tell me my weaknesses? Was the next step confession of my sins to God and congregation?

Then I became angry. "What does this woman know?" I cried out, as if Jesus was still sitting next to me. "She is just an old, out of work, too much time on her hands, worrier, who was too timid to speak up at the Session meeting and now wants to take it out on me. I am not like this! This is not me!"

I was defending something. I remembered Jesus words, "Whenever you feel insulted, there is an image involved." I remembered my teacher's instruction, "Pay attention. Look to yourself. Whenever you feel insulted, there is an image involved." What image was at play? Perhaps my image of myself as a pastor was insulted.

Reacting, I wrote a long accusatory reply to the email. History proved that personal emails had yet to work for me. Email only has served me for dates, times, and numbers. I deleted the email and tried again with a simple response, "Can we meet this week?"

During the night, I awoke about two o'clock and stayed awake for two hours. My mind was racing. I was having conversations in my head with the elder. In my imaginary dialogues, I explained all my behavior which might have been misinterpreted. Images of myself surfaced and argued with images I had of the elder. A committee meeting of images conducted itself in my head. The images of me tried to show how the decision by the Session was an expedient one. I talked over and over about procedure, responsibility, and the roles of pastor, elder, and congregation. Over and over the conversations went, without stopping. Exhausted, I finally fell back asleep.

The next day...I received a reply from the angry elder. She agreed to meet with me later in the week.

Movement:
From justifying images of self to a self beyond images.

Stepping Stone:
*When looking at others, remember, how you judge another
says more about you than it does about the other.
Use your judgments of others to learn about yourself.*

Consider the following story. Do the man's judgments of his
neighbor's son say more about the man or the boy next door?

*There once was a man who lost his axe. He looked around his yard for
the lost axe. While looking, his eyes fell upon his neighbor's son. He looked
suspicious to the man. The man watched the boy and, to him, every action of
the boy cried out of his guilt. The way he walked, his manner of speaking,
even the expression on his face seemed to indicate the boy's guilt. The man
was convinced beyond a shadow of a doubt that he had discovered what must
have happened to his axe.*

*On the way to confront the boy's father of the crime of the stolen axe, he
happened to see the axe leaning against his fence by his gate, right where he
left it.*

*Looking again at his neighbor's son, he noticed how innocent the boy
seemed. There was nothing at all in the boy's behavior or appearance that
suggested to the man that he had been a thief.*

The man was suspicious and thus saw the boy in an image
created by the suspicion. Anais Nin concluded, *We don't see things as
they are, we see them as we are.* If you want to see yourself, see how you
look at another person. When I ranted about the elder in my
congregation, the emotion the email stirred in me gave me an
excellent opportunity to learn about myself, to take a look inside, if I
was bold enough to look.

When have your emotions stirred this past week? What was the
focal event? What did you find (or would you have found) by being
bold enough to look inside yourself instead of focusing your energies
outward?

Stepping Stone:
When you feel insulted, look for the injured self image.

In the following story, imagine you are the student. How would you react?

A teacher was sharing with her students on how tightly held images can run our lives and shape our behaviors. One student raised his hand to ask a question. She acknowledged him. He stood up and said, "I don't agree that I have any images of self, nor do I think I hold tightly to them at all. I think I am free of self images."

She pointed her finger at him angrily and shouted, "Sit down, you bastard!"

The student was livid, he yelled back, "How can you consider yourself an enlightened person? You are no teacher! You ought to be ashamed of yourself."

The teacher replied, "Please forgive me, I was carried away. I don't know what came over me. You are right."

The man calmed down. She then told him, "Notice how at a single word of insult from me, a tempest flared inside you. Then, with an apology, the emotions calmed down. The emotions you felt are rooted in your images of self. Without a strongly held, unseen image of self, my insult would have no meaning, but because you hold tightly to your image, you are easily insulted because your tightly held image is easily threatened. Only images can be insulted. The self can never be."

Anytime there is a feeling of insult, there is an image at play. What image do you think the student had of himself? What do you think his image felt he deserved from his teacher?

Here is Thurber's quote again. This time I added my intro. Read it. (*When you feel insulted, don't*) look back in anger or forward in fear, but around in awareness.

How would my experience with my elder have changed had I taken his advice?

How will you respond differently the next time you feel insulted if you take Thurber's advice?

Stepping Stone:
When you feel insulted, respond don't react.
You can choose how you respond.

J. Krishnamurti wrote of our ability to not react when we feel insulted, but respond...

If my wife calls me an idiot, will I listen to her without forming an image? Or will it be the old tradition, habit, conditioning, the response of image-making? You follow? She calls me an idiot, but there is no image-making. Is that possible? Or when she flatters me, which is the same thing, the other side of the coin. Shall we go into this? That is, my wife calls me an idiot because I said or did something which she didn't like. Thought is conditioned, so the immediate response is an image. I am not an idiot. There is an image. Now can I listen to her – please find out – can I listen to her without that response? Which does not mean with indifference. Can I listen to her when she says, "Darling, you are marvelous" – which is another image? Can I listen to her, both when she calls me an idiot and when she calls me marvelous, without storing, without registering it?...The mechanism of the brain is to register. Right? It is registering. And it is so conditioned that it registers "idiot" immediately. Or when she says what a marvelous person I am, "marvelous" is registered. Now can there be no registering, when she calls me an idiot or she calls me marvelous? Which doesn't mean I become indifferent, hard, and callous. Now I can only do that – please listen – I can only not register, that is only possible, when I give my complete attention to what she says. Whether she calls me an idiot or marvelous, when I pay complete attention, there is no registering.[1]

What can you do to help yourself respond instead of react when you feel insulted?

Stepping Stone:
Let go of your images and look for liberation.

Letting go of images helps us find liberation. Anthony De Mello has written many books on awakening to life. One way he cited to

---

[1] J. Krishnamurti, <u>To Be Human</u>, p. 25.

awaken to our lives is by finding life beyond our images. For De Mello, life beyond images is liberating. He wrote...

What I'm about to say will sound a bit pompous, but it's true. What is coming could be the most important minutes in your lives. If you could grasp this, you'd hit upon the secret of awakening. You would be happy forever. You would never be unhappy again. Nothing would have the power to hurt you again. I mean that, nothing. It's like when you throw black paint in the air, the air remains uncontaminated. You never color the air black. No matter what happens to you, you remain uncontaminated. You remain at peace. There are human beings who have attained this, what I call being human. Not this nonsense of being a puppet, jerked about this way and that way, letting events or other people tell you how to feel. So you proceed to feel it and you call it being vulnerable. Ha! I call it being a puppet. So you want to be a puppet? Press a button and you're down; do you like that? But if you refuse to identify with any of those labels (or images), most of your worries cease....

...understand who "I" is, and you'll never be the same again, never. Nothing will be ever able to touch you again and no one will ever be able to hurt you again. You will fear no one and you will fear nothing.

"Nothing will be able to hurt you again," sounds strong, when we understand how much pain our images cause us, it makes sense.

The Enlightenment of Jesus:

In Luke chapter 9, we get a sense what an image free life might be like in the midst of image bound, easily insulted people.

Luke 9: *[51] When the days drew near for (Jesus) to be taken up, he set his face to go to Jerusalem. [52] And he sent messengers ahead of him. On their way they entered a village of the Samaritans to make ready for him; [53] but they did not receive him, because his face was set toward Jerusalem. [54] When his disciples James and John saw it, they said, "Lord, do you want us to command fire to come down from heaven and consume them?" [55] But he turned and rebuked them.*

In this passage, everyone seems to feel insulted but Jesus. The Samaritans felt insulted because Jesus was looking toward Jerusalem. (Samaritans and Jews each saw themselves as greater than the others.) The Samaritans saw Jesus' nod toward Jerusalem as lifting up Jews over Samaritans. Jesus' disciples felt insulted because the Samaritans didn't welcome Jesus. The disciples felt so insulted they wanted to call down fire to consume all the Samaritans – a wonderful metaphor for anger. Both the Samaritans and the disciples had images that were easily challenged. Jesus, on the other hand, did not feel insulted. What was different? Jesus had no image of self to defend. His lack of image allowed him to be present with both, to feel the need to react to either, but be present, be himself, not a false self, but an authentic self.

Earlier in the gospel, Jesus says in Luke 6: [27] *"But I say to you that listen, love your enemies, do good to those who hate you,* [28] *bless those who curse you, pray for those who abuse you...* [32] *"If you love those who love you, what credit is that to you?"* The normal pattern is to love those who reinforce our self images and hate those who challenge them. However, those who love their enemies can love those who challenge their images of self likely because they, like Jesus, don't have those images that are easily threatened or need to be proved.

Compassion is a big part of Jesus' life and the life he encourages. Living with the goal of justifying our self image or self images, we will only see those images, focusing, though not very well, only on ourselves. When we let go of the image, when we no longer need to justify them, then compassion is possible. We can put others center stage, listen to them, care for them, be present and patient with them. Authentic relating becomes possible when the masks fall away.

Epilogue

I met with the elder from the church who sent me the email. In our meeting, she used much of the same language from the email. She accused me of being *immature, controlling,* and *micromanaging.* I breathed deeply and just let the accusations roll by. I didn't allow any of my images needing justification to surface. I simply listened.

After a few minutes, surprisingly, I didn't feel any anger. I didn't feel much of anything, just calm.

Without the surfacing images, though she spoke about me, I heard her on a deeper level. I observed. I also thought of previous observations. She had been a part of the church for thirty five years.

Her children grew up in the church, but recently had moved away for college and beyond. Her husband had been diagnosed with cancer six months earlier.

I didn't refute any of the accusations, I simply made one comment in a question about what I had been hearing, "The tree is an important symbol to you of the stability of the church?"

She responded, "Yes. I have leaned on this church through many changes. I am continuing to lean on this church. When I look at the front of the church, I just can't imagine it without the tree there..."

She went on to talk about the changes in her family and in her life. We ended the meeting in tears and prayer.

Reflection:

Read the following quotes. How does each relate to the steps toward enlightenment described in this chapter?

People of the world don't look at themselves,
and so they blame one another.
Rumi

Everything that irritates us about others
can lead us to an understanding of ourselves.
Carl Jung

It is as though you have an eye
That sees all forms
But does not see itself.
This is how your mind is.
Its light penetrates everywhere
And engulfs everything,
So why does it not know itself?
Foyan

As long as a man stands in his own way,
everything seems to be in his way.
Ralph Waldo Emerson

He who knows others is learned. He who knows himself is wise.
Lao Tzu

The truth is that our finest moments
are most likely to occur when we are feeling
deeply uncomfortable, unhappy, or unfulfilled.
For it is only in such moments,
propelled by our discomfort,
that we are likely to step out of our ruts
and start searching for different ways or truer answers.
Scott Peck

We study people carefully for two main reasons:
in order to understand them
and fully experience our exchange with them,
or in order to feel ourselves superior.
John Gardner

Now what?

On the next chart, make a list of your roles. For example: child, parent, spouse, employer, employee (which may have many roles depending on your job).

Beside each role, list the different self images, or selves, you see that come out in you based on the situation.

Beside each self, write adjectives.
For example, here are some of mine as a minister.

ROLE	IMAGES	ADJECTIVES
Minister	Preacher	Authoritative, likes to be right, persuasive, confident, speaker
	Pastor	Patient, accepting, wants everyone to get along, listener
	Counselor	Wise, perceptive
	CEO	Organized, visionary
	Site Manager	Responsible

Now, you try. Don't forget relational roles: parent, child, spouse, sibling, etc.

If this exercise is difficult, once you list your roles, write the type of clothes that go with each. For example, in my preacher role I am likely to wear a tie, in my pastor role a sweater. In what way do the clothes make (or help create) the image? How are the clothes outfitted (or serve as costumes) to create each role? Use a separate sheet of paper if you need to.

ROLE	IMAGES OR PERSONAS	ADJECTIVES

Jesus accused the Pharisees of being 'hypocrites', a term used for actors. In what way might Jesus say you are acting out a role different from your true self?

How can you commit to a more authentic life this week?

Encounter Four:
Images of Self

Do I contradict myself?
Very well then I contradict myself.
(I am large, I contain multitudes.)
Walt Whitman

The next time I saw Jesus, it was late afternoon. I was tired. I hadn't slept well the night before. The children were doing their homework. Carrie was checking email. I was hiding in our bedroom beneath the comfort of blankets and the hum of reruns. After a brief scan of the channels, I settled for some mindless *Seinfeld* hoping a short nap might not be far off.

The show was just beginning. Jerry Seinfeld was out on stage at a comedy club.

I never get enough sleep. I stay up late at night, 'cause I'm Night Guy. Night Guy wants to stay up late. "What about getting up after five hours sleep? Oh, that's Morning Guy's problem. That's not my problem, I'm Night Guy. I stay up as late as I want." So you get up in the morning, you're exhausted, groggy. "Ooooh I hate that Night Guy!" See, Night Guy always screws Morning Guy. There's nothing Morning Guy can do. The only thing Morning Guy can do is try and oversleep often enough so that Day Guy loses his job and Night Guy has no money to go out anymore.

The sudden silence of the television startled me. From my half sleep haze I looked up. *Seinfeld* the show still played on, but Seinfeld the man was changing. Same body, same clothes, but his face altered. Jerry quickly became Jesus. He turned, stepped down from the stage and closer to the screen. He looked at me.

"Did I wake you?" he asked.

"No," I said. "Jesus, what are you doing on television?"

"Seinfeld's monologue has an important lesson for you, a life changing lesson. I didn't want you to miss it."

"Seinfeld?" I asked. "Seinfeld has an important lesson?"

"In this world, teachers abound," Jesus replied. "Opportunities to learn are everywhere. There is no shortage of teachers and teachable moments. The only shortage is students."

I then realized I was talking to the television. I looked around the room and into the hallway making sure no young eyes were watching me. I even looked out the window. I don't know who I thought might have been in my yard looking in, but I checked anyway.

"Are you worried about what others think?" Jesus asked.

I was. He obviously knew it, so I said nothing.

"Afraid that someone might think you're crazy?" Jesus asked.

Again I didn't reply, but I did turn my focus back on Jesus. I tried to regain his attention so that I didn't get a lecture against worrying about what others think. "Okay, my sitcom Savior, speak ahead. This student is listening."

"I'm here to encourage you to pay attention to the lesson from this Seinfeld episode. Comedians observe life, a habit more preachers should have. In this comedian's observations is an important lesson for you about who you are and what you do. Did you hear it?"

I thought back to the monologue before Jerry transformed to Jesus. I had seen the show a couple of times before, "Night Guy...Morning Guy?" I asked.

"Yes," Jesus said, "like the monologue, you have Night Guy and Morning Guy."

"Okay," I said agreeing without understanding.

"Night Guy sets the alarm clock. Morning Guy curses and hits the top of the clock," Jesus said.

I nodded.

"Night Guy and Morning Guy aren't your only personalities. You have many more," Jesus said.

I attempted to think of other guys I might have, but came up blank. I asked, "Dusk Guy and Dawn Guy?"

"Apparently Funny Guy," Jesus said not appreciating my attempt at humor. "You have Pastor Guy, Preacher Guy, Parent Guy, Twenty Year Old Guy, Compassionate Guy, Fix-it Guy, Successful Guy and many many many more."

"I do?" I asked again. "I have a Preacher Guy?"

"Sure," Jesus said. "Preacher Guy even has his own preacher voice."

"No," I said. I resisted the idea. I have noticed other preachers with very clear and distinctive preacher voices that felt to me like the combination of a car salesman and a bull horn, more like politician than pastor. "I don't have a preacher voice, do I?"

"Don't be surprised that you haven't noticed it," Jesus said. "Sleeping people are seldom aware of the personalities that come from their self images or the behaviors that they produce. Have you never noticed that the less confidence you have in what you are saying, the louder your preacher voice gets? Have you never noticed the less you feel like you know what you're speaking about the more authoritative your tone? You sound like you're impersonating Mr. Gilreath, your principal from seventh grade."

"No!" I declared. "Not really?"

"Let me hear you say - YE-ES!" Jesus laughed. Apparently Jesus found himself much funnier than he found me.

The Seinfeld scene changed. Jerry Jesus was walking around inside Seinfeld's apartment as he talked to me. "Each of these many, and I do mean many, guys, and the personalities they produce is rooted in an image you have of yourself. Remember our talk on self image?'"

I nodded.

"You have not just one image of self, but many - many self images. Beyond all the images, you do have a self. To sense your greater self, you must wake up to all the images and see them for what they are, products of your imagination, but you don't recognize them as images because you're still living your life much asleep."

"What do these images have to do with me sleeping?" I asked.

"People who are asleep can't tell the difference between an image and reality. Let me show you what I mean. Last night you had a very vivid dream."

"Yes, I did," I said. "I dreamed I was falling."

"At what point did you realize it was just a dream?" Jesus asked.

"I must have bounced on the bed or something, because I was suddenly jarred awake. When I woke up I knew I had been only dreaming, but while I was asleep I thought it was real." I replied.

"When you awoke, did you notice your body?" Jesus asked.

"My heart raced. I breathed heavily."

"Your body reacted as if you were actually falling,"

"Yes," I said.

"So," Jesus continued, "during the dream, at any time, were you aware falling was just an illusion, only an image in your mind?" Jesus asked.

"No," I said, "it felt very real."

"But it wasn't real," Jesus said.

"No, only a dream."

"An image," Jesus said.

"An image," I agreed.

"An illusion," Jesus said.

"An illusion," I agreed.

"When you are asleep, you don't recognize the dreamed image as an illusion. Falling Guy was only a dreamed image. When you awoke, you realized the distinction between dreaming and waking, image and reality. Are you aware that there are different levels to sleep – from a deep sleep to a shallow sleep?"

"Yes," I said. "I didn't sleep well last night, if that's what you mean."

"Exactly," Jesus said. "On a night you have a deep sleep you awake rested. On a night when you have a shallow sleep, you feel tired. In a similar manner, just like there are levels to sleep, there are levels to being awake, from slightly awake to fully awake. The semi awake, or sleep walking you, has just as difficult a time separating image from reality as the sleeping you did last night when you dreamed you were falling. The semi awake you contains images that are no more real than Falling Guy in your dream. Preacher guy, Parent Guy, Twenty Year Old Guy, Fix-it Guy, Pastor Guy are all dreamed up images. They aren't real, but they seem real to you until you are aware of them as illusions."

"How many images do I have?" I asked.

"Do you remember the gospel story of the man who lived in the tombs?"

"The guy with all the demons?" I asked.

"Do you remember what he said his name was when I asked?" Jesus inquired.

"Legion. He said, 'My name is Legion, for we are many.'"[2]

"Right," Jesus said. "That's you. You are many. Personality after

---

[2] Mark 5:9

personality. Image after image. Identity after identity. Many facsimiles. Many 'I's. Your idea of a unified 'I', one self image, one personality, one you, is false. The term, 'self image,' is deceptive for you have not one self image but many images of self, not one personality but many personalities, not one 'I', but many 'I's dependent upon role and situation. Each of these images of self can forge a life of its own shaping your mood, attitude, and actions. You have many images, many selves, many voices. You are legion for you are many."

I was stunned like the patient just given a cancer diagnosis. I didn't like the idea of multiple selves inside of me. I was quiet. Jesus waited.

"What should I do?" I asked.

"Just see," Jesus said. "Illusions only have power when they aren't seen for what they truly are, images. This week, just pay attention to some of the images of self that you have. Just see them. You'll be amazed at the difference just seeing them in yourself and others will make. Do you remember the man who lived in the tombs at the end of the story."

"He felt better?" I asked.

"As Mark and Luke say, "He was in his 'right mind.'"

Jesus smiled. The television went dark and Jesus was gone.

Movement:
From many images of self to the indivisible self.

Stepping Stone:
Remember that you are not one "I" but many.

Theodore Nottingham wrote...

We are not one person. There is no "I am," but many "I's" coming from numerous places within us. There is the "I" who is in command when it is hungry. There is the "I" who is in a bad mood, there is the "I" that loves to read poetry, and on and on. This work enables us to look at this phenomenon while it is happening. In the state of sleep, we just assume that we always act as the same person. Inner knowledge tells us that we are made up of many disconnected, fragmentary facets without unity.

...We say "I" to each activity in our mind: "I hate this...I am this...I want this." But this flood of constant response and talk in our brain is nothing more than life acting on our personality and our personality responding to it. We can form in ourselves, in our own psychology, a little bit of awareness that can stand back from that torrent of thought and activity and simply see—without response to it, without judgment or justification.

This seeing allows us to recognize that in one moment we are this "I", yesterday we were another "I". Life impacts us and our personality responds. That little bit of "observing I" within us will grow and become more powerful. Eventually it will lead to our "true I" where we will have the power to be more than merely reactions.

How do you feel your true "I" is different from your many images?

Stepping Stone:
In different locations, look for your different images of self.

One way images show up is when we take on different personalities, personas, or images in different settings, groups, or locations. If you are one person here, and another there, then there are images at play. These multiple images are easy to see, especially in people facing new situations, like newlyweds, like this couple...

One evening, I met with a couple I had married six months prior. They had just returned from visiting her parents and wanted to talk about it.

"So, you guys are having a problem," I said.

"I'll say," he said.

"It's really not that big of a deal," she said.

"Not to you," he said.

I took a breath and gave the tension a moment to clear the air.

"When did it start?" I asked.

"It started on our trip back home, right when we arrived," she said.

"Home?" he blurted out. "Home?" Looking to me he asked, "Shouldn't her home be with me and not her parent's house?"

"You know what I mean," she said to me. "We went back to my parent's house, where I grew up. My old home."

"So," I said, "something happened when you went to visit at your parent's house. Have you been back, since you got married?"

"No," he said. "Not together. She's been twice without me, but this is the first time together."

"But we went several times before we got married," she said.

"So," I said looking at the husband who seemed to be the most upset by the visit, "what happened when you got to your in-laws' house?"

"It's really nothing," she interrupted.

"It's not any one thing," he said. "It's several."

"For example?" I asked.

"It was how she talked to her father."

"How did she talk to her father?"

"Like she was twelve years old again," he said. "As soon as she saw him, she ran up to him, jumped up, hugged him, he lifted her off the ground, and she started this 'baby talk'."

"I did not use baby talk," she said.

"You felt uncomfortable watching how she hugged her father and hearing how she spoke to him," I said.

"Wouldn't you, if your wife jumped into her father's arms like a little girl and started using baby talk?"

"I didn't jump into his arms," she said. "And I didn't talk like a baby."

I looked toward her, "Can you tell me a time on this trip when you felt uncomfortable?"

"I felt uncomfortable when we got there. We had been arguing before we arrived, and as soon as we saw my parents, you could just feel the tension coming off of him. They're my family, too, shouldn't I be able to..."

I interrupted, "Can you think of another time, besides the car ride and your arrival when you felt uncomfortable?"

"Yes," she said. "I was in the kitchen, talking with my mother. I was in the middle of the room, my mother leaning against the counter. He walked in behind me. He threw his arms around my shoulders and hugged me tight, while I was talking to my mother! Then he kissed me."

"Kissed you?" I asked.

"On the back of my neck," she said.

"It wasn't a passionate kiss, just a little peck, a little 'I love you' peck," he said.

"And you felt uncomfortable," I said to her.

"Yes. At home, fine, even out in public, that would be okay, but not in front of my mother, not in the kitchen."

"Was there another time when you felt uncomfortable while in your in laws' home?" I asked shifting focus back to him.

"There sure was," he said. "A short time after we had arrived, after watching my wife become a little girl in her father's arms, I carried our suitcase upstairs to her old bedroom. I walked in and felt nauseous."

"Nauseous?" I asked.

"Nauseous," he responded. "The room was painted pink. Her high school pom poms were on display on the dresser, and a picture of her and her prom date on the night table by her bed. Nauseous. I mean, I was going to sleep with my wife in this room, the room of a teenager."

"It's my room," she replied.

"It is the room of who you used to be," he corrected, "not who you are."

"Being at her parent's home, you felt frustrated, like you married an adult but came home with a teenager?"

"I think that's the feeling," he said.

"And you," I said turning to her, "were caught between roles, you were expected by your parents to be the daughter of their memories while your husband wanted you to be the wife of his dreams. Each apart was fine, but together irreconcilable."

"Yes," she said. "I felt torn in two, like I couldn't win. I couldn't satisfy them both. I was lost somewhere in the middle. Not sure I'm either of those roles, daughter or wife, or maybe both. It was confusing."

"Is there anything we can do to improve our relationship?" he asked.

"The tension will likely lessen over time. You probably can help the situation by encouraging your parents to turn your old room into a guest room instead of a shrine to your high school years."

"Give up my room?" she asked.

"Yes," I said.

"I'm not ready," she said.

When personalities change with location, images are involved. How many other images do you think the couple in this story had? Were each different at their jobs than they were here?

What about you? How are you different in your varying locations? Do you have a different persona for each place?

Stepping Stone:
Remember, self images don't like to age.
To mature, let go of immature images.

I got a tragic call from an old friend in South Carolina, a man about my age at the time, early forties. He confessed that he had been having an affair with an office staffer. He described her as young, single, in her twenties. As I listened to his story, I remembered the saying ministers tend to use about church life and counseling, "What it's about is seldom what it's about." This seemed especially true with this friend. To me, the affair didn't seem to be about sex. He was aging. To deny his reality, he had to deny his family. He had a much younger than actual image of self. His wife was aging. The addition of a second child meant more responsibility. His Twenty Year Old Guy couldn't live with that supporting cast, so he sought to weave his drama around another younger significant other as co-star for his self created drama of being twenty. "She makes me feel young," he admitted. "How long do you think this will last?" I asked. "I don't know," he replied. "I try not to think about it."

Though not a dominant self image for me, my Twenty Year Old Guy shows up when I go to the YMCA. Sometimes more than others, like one day, after warming up on the elliptical trainer, I went to the weight room. I went to the leg press machine and started pulling some weight from the stacks to place on the machine. Behind me, on the shoulder press machine, one of two late high school early college guys spoke, "Excuse me," he said. "We were about to use that machine."

"About to?" I asked. "There is no about to, only you are, or you aren't. It looks to me like you're working over there." If I would have been a dog, a cat, or a large squirrel, my fur on the back of my neck would have raised up.

"Yeah," he replied.

Continuing to mark my territory, I put an extra forty-five pound plate on each side. Pleased with the weight I lifted, I finished my set and locked the weight in place. I then found that not only did the weight lock in place, but also did my thighs. I got up and walked unbendingly out of the weight room like a salty pirate with two wooden legs. Apparently, I was finished with the leg press machine and left it for the young.

In the locker room, I considered what image I was reinforcing. I, too, had an image of myself as a twenty year old I didn't want to let go. The younger males had entered my space. Twenty Year Old Guy sought to justify his existence by pushing the extra weight. However, upon completion, my forty year old legs could barely move.

I remembered another friend who recently had a similar epiphany lifting weights at the Y. A young woman surfaced his Twenty Year Old Guy and then smacked him to the ground. He thought her attractive and fantasized she thought the same of him. Then the alarm clock went off, the fantasy revealed for the illusion it was. He and she both walked toward the same exercise machine at the same time. "You go ahead," he said with self confident smile. Then she spoke, "Thank you..." and with one additional word leveled his fantasy world. She said, "Sir." "Thank you, sir." Twenty Year Old Guy was slain like an over sized turkey at Thanksgiving.

In my locker, I saw the work out journal I kept. At the end of work outs, I used to fill out a chart recording the weight I lifted, the laps I swam, or the miles and speed of my bicycle rides. The image I had of myself which called for the behavior could likely be called Improving Guy. I liked to think of myself as improving. The alternative terrified me. 'Who wants to be Aging Guy?' When I filled out the work out paper, if my times weren't better, my laps faster, my bike rides farther, or my weight heavier, I was disappointed. I wanted to see myself as constantly 'improving'. The alternative was clear. If not constantly improving, then constantly aging... and degenerating.

Stepping Stone:
See the images others present for what they are – images..
The image you deal with now
may not be the same image you encounter later.

In church work, I found that often, if someone is upset with me, waiting until another time (not long, just a few days) can get me an encounter with a different image, and thus, a different persona all together. This approach has helped me deal with conflict and achieve goals within our church community.

One of my favorite church members and volunteers is Tom. I know Tom. I love Tom. Tom was on the committee that hired me. Tom also headed up our capital drive for our building. Tom and I have worked together a lot, and I have a particular way that I like to work with Tom. With most of our leaders, I meet during the day, but Tom I always meet at night. With most leaders, I meet at the church, a coffee shop or restaurant, with Tom I always meet at his house. Here's why.

Tom, like the rest of us, has multiple selves. As a pastor, you want to know as many of the multiple selves of your church treasurer as you can, but, specifically, you want to know which ones are inclined to save money and which ones are inclined to spend money. Professionally, Tom is a banker. One of Tom's dominant guys is Banker Tom. Banker Tom protects money, which is very important for a church treasurer. I learned quickly that anytime a program was proposed that cost money and someone asked, "Tom is there enough money for...?" Banker Tom always said, "No." When members of the Session (our church board) would ask Tom about money, they would get frustrated with the consistent, "No, there is not enough money." They didn't know it was Banker Tom, and Banker Tom always say, "No," when it comes to spending money. I learned not to ask Tom a money question at Session because that would always get an answer from Banker Tom and only Banker Tom. I also learned not to ask Tom a money question over lunch because Banker Tom always goes to lunch. I did find, however, that if I went to Tom's house in the evening, when he was off work and not in his Banker Tom suit, then I found Bartender Tom. Bartender Tom, unlike Banker Tom, always says, "Yes." "Tom, can I have a beer?" "Yes, I'll get it." "Tom, can we spend money on a new program." "Yes. Sounds good to me." I like Banker Tom. But I love Bartender Tom. Bartender Tom says, "Yes."

If you don't like the image someone is presenting, wait until they are off work or until they go to work. Either way, you're likely to encounter a different person altogether, different approaches, different reactions, different values.

Stepping Stone:
Let go of deficient images.

We cause ourselves a lot of suffering. Especially when we choose deficient images like the following common images:

Just a... I know a man who, when younger, dropped out of high school and never went back. He became a painter. When we met, even though he had his own business, responsible for ten employees, he still felt badly because he never finished high school. When introduced and asked what he did, he would say, "I'm just a painter." *Just a...* was a dominant image for him.

Only a... I know a mother of three. Her husband worked out of town most of the week. She stayed home with her young children. When asked what she did, she said, "I'm only a housewife." On call twenty-four hours a day, nurturing and caring for the lives of three children, yet, she saw herself as "Only a housewife." *Only a...* was a dominant image for her.

Used to be..." I know a retired professor who was struggling with his loss of employment and with that loss a void in his sense of self. I could still hear him in my mind, "My life was clear before. I knew who I was. I had tenure. I had clout. Now, when people ask me what I do, I don't know what to say. All I can say is that 'I used to be a professor.'" *Used to be...* was his dominant image.

They each had images of self that society had demeaned: *Just a...,* *Only a...,* and *Used to be...,* those images were somehow, in their minds, less than human, and because of these images of who they should be and weren't, life itself seemed to insult them. These images cause many people lots of personal pain, yet they are very difficult to leave behind.

Do you suffer from any of these images? From others?

Stepping Stone:
Kill your self images. They won't die on their own.

Most pastors, me included, have a personality, which, if named, would be Fix-It Guy or Fix-It-Gal.

For me, if there was a problem around the church, I liked to think I could always fix it, or at least make it better. "David, we have a problem." "Great, let me fix it." "David, I have a personal problem." "Great, let me help fix it." "David, I need to get married." "Great, I can fix that for you." "David, I don't understand this Bible passage." "Great, I can fix that." "David, there is a toilet backed up." "I can fix that."

I like thinking of myself as a fix it, but living up to it, always being Mr. Fix It, is exhausting. I remember one time in particular. One Sunday morning, I encountered several people with various comments on problems at church: Sunday School attendance was down; the Coke machine was out of Diet Coke; one of the shrubs in the front lawn was dead; someone didn't like the book the Women of the Church group was using in their study; and others. With each comment, I felt responsible. I needed to make things right or else I wasn't Fix It Guy.

That afternoon, to add to my overwhelmed feeling, I went to see a couple struggling with cancer. The chemo therapy wasn't working. They asked me to pray for healing. They gave a look that pastors often get when medicine fails. I call it the "so, what you got?" look. They looked to me for some sort of connection to God which might do what science had failed to do. I left feeling powerless. I went home.

I was hoping my house would be an oasis. I was hoping for a little peace and quiet to calm my inner anxiety. My children didn't oblige my need for rest. My children were attempting to out quarrel the Middle East. Encountering their conflict, Fix It Guy said, "That's okay, I'm Fix It Guy. I'll show them a better way. Fix It Guy can fix it."

I spent time showing them how to communicate. "Own your feelings. Say, 'Nathan, when you pulled my hair I felt angry because it hurt my head.' Ask for what you want, 'Nathan, please don't pull my hair anymore. If you'd like me to play with you, just ask.'"

When lessons in communication were over, they smiled and left me. Soon, they were fighting again. In search of a world that could calm my inner turmoil, I succumbed to begging. Pathetic Parent came out. "Dad has had a rough day. Can you please try and get along for me?"

"Sure, Dad." Five minutes later. "Bam! Waaaah!"

My image of self as 'fix it' was dying inside. I couldn't change it, but I did see it. I saw the source of my pain. I was ready to abandon my children when they didn't help justify my image, my sense of power in the world. After all, "Who am I if I can't fix my family?" "If I can't 'fix' my children's relationships, how can I fix anything else? If I can't solve something so seemingly simple, what could I offer the family struggling with cancer?" The pain was tremendous. My image of myself as a "fix it" was dying in front of me.

The only way I have found to get release from my Fix It Guy image was to kill him. "Dearly Beloved, we are gathered here today to say goodbye to our friend, Fix It Guy..." As soon as I do, as soon as I let him go to the glory beyond, I feel my mind relax. I feel a sense of peace. I don't have to prove I am Fix-It Guy. I don't have to be, nor can I be, responsible for every little problem at the church or home. (If killing him sounds violent, don't worry, he keeps coming back.)

The Enlightenment of Jesus:

Jesus encountered a man with many images.

Mark 5: *They came to the other side of the sea, to the country of the Gerasenes.* [2] *And when he had stepped out of the boat, immediately a man out of the tombs with an unclean spirit met him.* [3] *He lived among the tombs; and no one could restrain him any more, even with a chain;* [4] *for he had often been restrained with shackles and chains, but the chains he wrenched apart, and the shackles he broke in pieces; and no one had the strength to subdue him.* [5] *Night and day among the tombs and on the mountains he was always howling and bruising himself with stones.* [6] *When he saw Jesus from a distance, he ran and bowed down before him;* [7] *and he shouted at the top of his voice, "What have you to do with me, Jesus, Son of the Most High God? I adjure you by God, do not torment me."* [8] *For he had said to him, "Come out of the man, you unclean spirit!"* [9] *Then Jesus asked him, "What is your name?" He replied, "My name is Legion; for we are many."* [10] *He begged him earnestly not to send them out of the country.* [11] *Now there on the hillside a great herd of swine was feeding;* [12] *and the unclean spirits begged him, "Send us into the swine; let us enter them."* [13] *So he gave them permission. And the unclean spirits came out and entered the swine; and the herd, numbering about two thousand, rushed down the steep bank into the sea, and were drowned in the sea.*

[14] *The swineherds ran off and told it in the city and in the country. Then people came to see what it was that had happened.* [15] *They came to Jesus and saw the demoniac sitting there, clothed and in his right mind...*

Jesus knew that the man was more than the legion which had taken over. In a similar fashion, Jesus knows we are all more than our legion of images that can torment us. To be freed from all the images is to come to a place like the man in the previous passage, *in our right mind.*

Jesus liberated the man by killing the images that tormented him. I do think killing our images is the appropriate metaphor. Jesus challenged (here from Mark 8) *"If any want to become my followers, let them deny themselves and take up their cross and follow me.* [35] *For those who want to save their life will lose it, and those who lose their life for my sake, and for the sake of the gospel, will save it."*

The passage can be read, *"If any want to become my followers, let them deny their selves (or their self images) take up their cross putting those images to death and follow me. For those who want to save their self images will lose their life and those who lose their images will find life.*

Whether killing, ending, or letting go of the image works for you, the only way to be free from them is to free yourself. Take up your cross, put an end to them. Try and save them, and you'll lose your life, not to mention your right mind, but let them go, and you can live, hopefully in a more sane fashion than when you were tortured by your images.

Reflection:

Read the following quotes. How does each relate to the steps toward enlightenment described in this chapter?

I do not know how to distinguish
between our waking life and a dream.
Are we not always living the life
that we imagine we are?
Henry David Thoreau

All the world's a stage,
And all the men and women merely players.
They have their exits and their entrances,
And one man in his time plays many parts,
His acts being seven ages.
Shakespeare

Know thyself.
Socrates

Know thy selves.
Jones

If you could get rid
of yourself just once,
The secret of secrets
Would open to you.
The face of the unknown,
Hidden beyond the universe
Would appear on the
Mirror of your perception.
Rumi

To be nobody-but-yourself in a world which is doing its best,
night and day, to make you everybody else –
means to fight the hardest battle which any human being can fight;
and never stop fighting.
ee cummings

Now what?

Think of times you felt praised recently. What images of yourself do you think felt affirmed by the praise?

Think of times you felt insulted recently. What images of yourself do you have that felt threatened by the insult?

How can you let go of your self image and connect with someone you've been distant from in the past?

Will you?

Encounter Five:
Images and Others

Man stands in his own shadow and wonders why it's dark.
Zen Proverb

Part One

I like to think of myself as a good father. Good fathers prepare their children for life, and good fathers prepare their sons... for sports.

So, with great pride, I watched as my son, Nathan, age five, took the field for his first soccer game. "Have a good game, son!" I yelled.

"Okay, Dad," he replied.

I envisioned him scoring one to two goals a game, for the first season.

The ball was kicked into play. Nathan ran with the pack, and then emerged with the ball. I beamed. "He's a natural," I said to an invisible crowd of dads who looked at me in admiration and envy. Then another child came and kicked the ball away from Nathan.

"Get the ball, son!" I yelled.

He didn't get the ball. He didn't move. He just stood there. Then he walked over to me on the sideline and cried out for justice, "Dad," he complained, "that kid took the ball from me."

Not sure of how to respond, I said, "Yes, that's how soccer is played."

"But Dad, it was my turn," Nathan said.

"In soccer..." I began.

"He didn't share," Nathan said.

'This is a problem,' I thought. 'We try to teach him to share, now he's confused.' "That's how soccer is played. You don't share in soccer. You get the ball and score," I said with enthusiasm on *score*. "Go and play!"

He ran back onto the field. He kept running after the ball but only where it used to be. After a while he gave up and ran around the field, arms outstretched. I think he was pretending to be a plane, a bird, or a very strange gorilla.

During his second season, he expanded his activities from soaring to socializing. Nathan loves making new friends. He saw the other team not as opponent but opportunity. He would run along side of them and not try and defeat them but meet them. "Hi, my name is Nathan. Do you like video games?" "Hi, my name is Nathan, would you like to come over to my house and play?"

"That's my boy..." I whispered to his mother, guilt ridden for not orienting him to the world of sports in a better fashion.

Weeks later, on a Friday night, at a birthday party at Chuckie Cheese, the kid-filled video game abounding pizza place with a large rat as a mascot, Nathan was enjoying himself. "Dad, I love Chuckie Cheese," he said. "Can we come back tomorrow?"

With the lights, buzzers, bells, and mass of children scurrying around at my feet, it took all the stamina I had to stay in the building that night. "Son," I started, "there is no way I am coming back to Chuckie Cheese tomorrow..." But then I thought about soccer. I had felt deficient dad, certain good dad would have instilled in his son a greater passion for the game of soccer. In what seemed right, good, and true at the time, I said to Nathan, "I'll tell you what, you score a goal at soccer tomorrow, and I'll bring you back to Chuckie Cheese."

"Okay, Dad," and he was off to play.

The next day, feeling a little remorse that I had bribed my son to try harder at soccer, I was hoping that maybe he'd forgotten, naïve I was.

The game started. His team scored a goal about two minutes after he was on the field. He ran over to me on the sideline. "Dad, we scored a goal. Can I go to Chuckie Cheese?"

"No, you have to score the goal," I replied.

"Okay, Dad," and he was off.

Two minutes later, in the pack and then he emerged with the ball. He dribbled it down the middle. Blew by two defenders with intensity I had never seen from him, and scored. "That's my boy!" I yelled.

He cheered. High fived his team mates, then ran to me. "Dad, are we going to Chuckie Cheese?"

I had no answer I could feel good about. Only one answer I could give. "Yes," I said.

The rest of the game, Nathan was back to flying around like an airplane, introducing himself to boys from the other team and inviting them over to his house to play.

After the game, the coach asked me, "What happened to Nathan? He was in the game in the first quarter, and then faded."

"Beat's me," I lied.

That afternoon, I was back at Chuckie Cheese, sitting at a table, watching my son run around playing video games and ski ball. That's when Jesus showed up, sitting in my booth.

He just looked at me and smiled. I smiled back. Then he spoke.

"Score a goal, and I'll take you to Chuckie Cheese?" he asked.

"Okay," I said, "definitely not my finest moment as a parent."

He was quiet. He just looked at me and smiled.

"Say something," I urged.

He just smiled.

I waited.

"Score a goal, and I'll take you to Chuckie Cheese," he said laughing.

"Stop laughing at me," I demanded.

"I'm not laughing at you," he said. "I'm laughing with you."

"But I'm not laughing," I said.

"Okay, then I'm laughing at you."

"Great," I said.

"Okay," Jesus offered, "let's see what we can learn from this. What did you learn about yourself."

"That I'm a lousy parent," I said.

"You think so?" he asked.

"Don't you?" I asked.

"Again, let's see what we can learn. Your bribe, was it more about you or about Nathan?"

"Me, I guess," I replied.

"You guess?" Jesus asked.

"Okay, me."

"What did you want?" Jesus asked.

"For Nathan to score a goal," I replied.

"Okay, why?"

"So I would feel better about myself as a parent," I said.

"So, Nathan scores, and you feel better," he summarized.

"Something like that," I agreed.

"You imagine yourself as a good parent. Part of that image includes Nathan doing well at soccer. The *If/Then* dynamic is set up. *If* you are a *good* parent *then* Nathan scores. And, if he doesn't, then you are a *bad* parent who didn't prepare his son. Is that it?"

"Something like it," I said.

"Remember the lesson after your bike accident?"

"Full minds create chaos?"

"What do you suppose your mind was full of here that could create chaos in your relationship with your son?"

"Images of myself as a good father?"

"Yes," he said. "What else?"

"Images of Nathan," I said.

"When observing your images," he instructed, "pay close attention to the adjectives you attribute to those images. Adjectives combined with images are dangerous because they dictate rigid expectations. Pay attention to adjectives like strong, weak, young, old, smart, stupid, capable, incapable, and the adjectives that cause you the most suffering of all... good and bad. Pay attention to how often you connect 'good' and 'bad' with your images of self and how much of your internal pain is rooted in those two adjectives. Because of your images, good father good son, you weren't paying attention to your son," Jesus said.

"What do you mean?" I asked.

"The image of yourself as a good parent kept you from actually seeing your son. Because of the image, all you could see was how he justified or challenged the image of Good Dad. Think about Nathan. If you were to make a list of the happiest children you know, where would Nathan place on that list?"

"Most of the time, he would rank first. Most of the time he is one of the happiest children I know."

"Think back to Nathan on swim team," Jesus instructed. What do you remember?"

I remembered Nathan, age five, in his first year of league swimming, was the youngest boy on the team. I remembered each time we came to pick him up from the pool, while the other kids swam, Nathan was carried in the arms of one of the assistant coaches, usually a girl around age twelve to fourteen. My son used his age, better than average smile, and droopy eyes to his advantage. He practiced much but swam little.

I remember during one meet, Nathan was swimming back stroke. There were six girls running along the side of the pool cheering for him, all the while, swimming on his back, he was smiling and waving. It wasn't a meet for Nathan, it was a parade. He got out of the pool and didn't ask, "What place did I come in?" or "What was my time?" but instead, "Where did the girls go?"

During the last meet, I took the camera. He was swimming free style, until he saw me. He stopped in the pool to wave.

"Happy or unhappy child?" Jesus asked.

"Usually happy," I replied.

"Then be careful what you teach him about soccer. You were instructing him not to be happy unless he's scoring goals. The truth was, with your image of Good Dad, it was you who wouldn't be happy without him scoring goals. The situation had little to do with Nathan at all."

"So," I asked, "images I have of others usually connect to an image I have of myself?"

"Right," Jesus said. "You can't begin to understand how you image anyone, until you first see your images of yourself. Once you see your images of yourself, then you can see the images you have of others. Pay attention not just to the images you have of yourself, but how you think of others. They are related."

"I will," I promised.

Jesus didn't disappear. Instead, he took some tokens from a cup on the table and walked over to play ski ball. I watched him for a while. I went and found Nathan to take him over to Jesus. Partly to have Nathan meet Jesus, partly to verify he was actually present at Chuckie Cheese. By the time I found Nathan, Jesus was gone.

Part Two
Three weeks later.

It was Easter Sunday. In the post worship, prenap phase, I sat back in my chair and closed my eyes. I felt good about my sermon. I had a lot of people tell me it was a 'good' one. I felt my goal had been accomplished. Easter always brings visitors. I wanted to preach such a good sermon that everyone would go home and call someone and tell them, "I heard a great sermon!" I felt I had come close.

Almost asleep, I heard a tap, tap, tap on the window.

I ignored it.

Then, tap, tap, tap.

I opened my eyes to see Jesus outside my window, in my back yard, tapping and smiling.

I went outside. He was sitting on the swing. I sat on the swing next to him.

"*Good* Easter sermon," he said.

There was something in his voice that disturbed me.

"Glad you liked it?" I said cautiously.

"That's what you wanted," he said, "a *good* sermon."

I can never tell when I'm being spoken to, or baited.

"Yes?" I said.

"Your goal was something other than preaching a good sermon," he said.

I was puzzled, "I didn't want to preach a good sermon?"

"Oh, you want to preach a good sermon, alright. But that's not what you want everyone telling their friends. You didn't want people calling others to say they heard a really good sermon, what you're hoping is for people to go home, call a friend or family member, and say they heard a really good preacher."

"What's the difference?" I asked.

"A good sermon is about the sermon. A good preacher is about you."

"About me?" I asked.

"Yes, about you. Your desires for Easter Sunday say a lot about you. They are the mirror to your personalities. Remember, observe yourself."

I thought back to my previous couple of visits with Jesus. He had shown me that I am not one I but many. I have many images of self. He showed me that they are illusions, dreams of a sleeping man. The one showing up today is Preacher Guy. I responded to Jesus, "Preacher Guy is trying to justify his existence by having everyone think he gave the best Easter sermon ever."

"Yes," said Jesus. "If you can think that the congregation thinks they heard a good sermon from a good preacher, then you can justify the image. Pay attention, let me clear something up. It's not really that you want people to think you're a good preacher, you want to think people think you're a good preacher."

"What's the difference?" I asked.

"Well, you actually know little about what goes on inside of other people's heads, even though you pretend that you do," Jesus told me.

"I don't?" I asked.

"No. You think you do, but those are just images. You're so asleep, you barely, if ever, see beyond your images of others, and they barely see beyond their images of you. You are worried about what others think of you. If you knew the truth, you'd be disappointed just how little time other people spend actually thinking of you. They actually think of you hardly at all. Like you, they are caught up in their own images. Take, for example, your image of the new family that just joined the church,"

"Roger and Jean," I said. "I like Roger, he's a good guy."

"You just met Roger," Jesus said.

"Yes," I said.

"Yet you think Roger is a good guy," Jesus said.

"Yes," I said. "Isn't he?"

"Whether or not Roger is a good guy, a nice guy, or a sadistic hedonist who slaughters bunnies for sport is not the point," said Jesus. "The point is that you think Roger is a good guy when you just met him. Do you know why you think Roger is a good guy?"

"No," I admitted.

"You think Roger is a good guy because your experience with Roger supports the image you have about yourself as a good preacher. Do you remember what Roger said about you as a preacher when they joined the church?" Jesus asked.

I did remember. "Roger said that I was the best preacher of all the pastors he has ever had."

"Right," said Jesus. "We've already established that you want to think others think you are a good preacher."

"Right," I said.

"You like Roger because he strokes the image you want to have of yourself. If the day comes Roger says he thinks you stink as a preacher, will you still say, 'Roger is a good guy?'"

"Probably not..." I confessed. "So I think Roger is a good guy because I felt good hearing what Roger said about me. If I had a bad feeling connected to Roger then I'd likely say he's a jerk?"

"Highly likely."

"Do you know what I want from you?" Jesus asked.

"Apparently not to try to be a good preacher," I said.

"Trying to be a good preacher is what is keeping you from growing as a preacher," he said.

"What do you want from me?" I asked.

"Nothing," he said.

"Nothing?" I asked.

"Nothing," he said. "I want you to give me nothing. And for you, that's going to be one of the toughest things I could ask of you."

He was gone. I was sitting in the swing by myself.

My son, Nathan, came out. "Dad, you want me to push you?" he asked.

Movement:
From attempting to see others in ways that justify self images to letting go of self images and being fully present with others.

Stepping Stone:
*Our unseen images will shape what we want from others.
Pay attention. See how, as your self images change,
what you want from others changes.*

To reinforce my image of myself as 'good dad', I wanted for my son to do well in soccer and score goals. To reinforce my image of myself as 'good preacher,' I wanted members of my congregation to tell me I preached 'good sermons.' How we see others is largely rooted in unseen images we are trying to reinforce.

The result is we interact with others but don't see them at all. We only see how they fit our image reinforcements or not. Over time, we encounter another problem. As our images change, what we want, need, and expect from others changes. People who used to bring us pleasure as they reinforced our desired images may challenge our new quest to support a fresh image. This happens often when dating moves to marriage. Often, what attracts you to someone while dating may be the very behaviors you later abhor. For example, I used to regularly see for counseling a disgruntled husband. Jim came to see me about every six months. The presenting problem was always the same, how to "deal with his wife."

Jim met Karen when they were both in college. Karen was on the side of the road looking, as he described her, "like a lost lamb." She had run out of gas. He took her to the gas station and back to her car. He left her with two gallons of gas and his phone number in case she ever needed his help.

She apparently needed his help quite a bit. He helped her through her college science classes and in dealing with her roommate. He bailed her out a couple of times when she didn't have money for her rent.

On this visit, he came to see me, frustrated, because she had run out of gas again, but this time on the highway with their two young children, ages three and five, with her. She had called him during a meeting with a company with whom he was discussing doing some consulting work. When he didn't pick up the first time, she called right back, their signal for an emergency. When we sat down together, he was fuming.

"She's so helpless," he said. "Not only did she run out of gas, but I found out she hasn't had the oil changed in the van in 7,000 miles and she just over maxed the credit card."

I thought back to our previous visits. I knew there must be an image at play for both of them, but I couldn't see what it was. I decided to go back to the beginning and explore the start of their relationship.

"Running out of gas and needing your help is a pattern with her, isn't it?" I asked.

"Yes, among other things," he said.

"How many times has she run out of gas?"

"Four or five," he replied.

"Counting before you were married?"

"Yes," he said.

"That's how you met, she was on the side of the road. She had run out of gas."

"Yes, that's right."

"You stopped and helped her?" I asked.

"Yes," he said.

"You left her with your phone number?"

"Right," he said.

"What did you feel when you helped her that day?"

"What did I feel?" he asked.

"Yes, were you attracted to her? Did you feel powerful, useful, manly? You must have felt something. You left her your phone number."

"I was glad to help her out."

"What else?"

"I thought she was cute. I wanted to spend more time with her."

"You must have liked how you felt with her to want to see her again. Can you described it some more?"

"I helped her. I like helping."

"When you started your relationship," I said, "you were sort of the continual helper and she was the helpee. Is that right?"

"I guess so," he said.

"It worked for you then," I said.

"Yes," he said.

"It felt good?" I asked.

"Yes," he said.

"Jim, you are a business consultant, isn't that sort of a helper?"

"I guess so. I try and help companies."

"In what way?"

"Companies that are struggling, I come in and help them reexamine their corporate structures, help them make changes to be more efficient and more profitable."

"You are a corporate rescuer," I said.

"Rescuer is a little strong," he said.

"You liked helping Karen when you were dating, she ran out of gas and you liked helping her. Now she runs out of gas, and you're frustrated. What's changed?"

"It's not cute anymore. She's an adult. She should be able to manage better."

We talked further. I helped him with some communication skills he could use with Karen about what his needs were. I saw in them a common principle about marriage: the things which attract while dating can be the things that annoy and frustrate the most when married. Dating, she was needy, and he needed to be needed. As a helper or rescuer, he was attracted to Karen. Her neediness justified his self image as a rescuer. However, after years of marriage, her consistent neediness doesn't justify his image as a rescuer any more. If he's a rescuer, she should get rescued. If she doesn't get rescued, then he's not a rescuer.

Jim struggled with his unseen images. Karen had reinforced one of his primary self images while they were dating, but once they got married, what he wanted from her changed. The very behaviors he found attractive while dating were frustrating him as her husband.

How have your images changed over time? Is there anyone who used to reinforce your sense of self earlier in your life who now frustrates it?

Stepping Stone:
See self expectations.

Imagine you are the samurai in the following story:

A samurai went to see the local priest. "I have mastered being a warrior, now I would like to master being a priest."

"You want to be a priest?" the priest asked the samurai.

"Yes," said the samurai.

"Great," said the priest. "First, let's have a cup of tea."

The two men knelt at the table. The priest put out two cups. First, one to the samurai and then one to himself, then he started filling the samurai's cup. He poured until it overflowed, over the brim, onto the table and then onto the samurai. All the while, the priest whistled.

The samurai felt insulted. He jumped up, drew his sword and raised it over his head to strike the priest. The priest then said, "You are not ready to learn the way of peace. You are not ready to learn at all. You are like this cup. You are so full of yourself that you have no room to learn anything."

Why did the priest bring out the samurai's anger? What image of the Samurai is at play?

Read the story again.

Given what you know about samurais, which doesn't have to be much, what adjectives would distinguish a 'good' samurai from a 'bad' one in your mind?

The samurai's primary image of himself was as a 'good' warrior. He lived thinking and trying to think of himself as a 'good' warrior. This image drove his actions and expectations. Not only did it shape his behavior, but how he expected others to respond. In his mind, if he was a 'good' warrior, then everyone would treat him with respect and fear. Because of this image, anyone who insulted him threatened his image of self. To him, this threat to image felt like a physical threat. He was ready to kill the priest because he felt the priest had insulted/challenged his image of himself as a warrior when he poured tea on him. A 'good' warrior instilled respect and fear in everyone. If he was a good warrior then the priest wouldn't treat him like this. By pouring hot tea on him, the priest was not treating him with the respect and fear, that in his mind, a 'good' warrior deserved. In order to protect his image of self, he was ready to kill or injure the priest to make sure the priest 'respected' and feared him and thereby supporting his image of self.

The awake priest could see the self image of the samurai. The priest challenged him to let go of his false image of self by attacking the image, bringing it to the surface, so the samurai might have an opportunity first to see it and then to let go of it so that he might be open to learning.

Stepping Stone:
*Drop labels of 'good' and 'bad'
from the way you look at yourself and others.*

My mother taught me there were 'bad' words, I won't list them here. For a good list, see George Carlin's *Seven Words You Can't Say on Television,* they were also the seven words this seven year old couldn't say in the Jones' home. Through the enlightenment of Jesus, I have discovered some new dirty words: *good, bad, should, have to, ought to,* and *must.*

There is only one instance in the gospels where someone calls Jesus 'good', and he doesn't take it as a compliment. The incident is the encounter with the one the Bible calls *the rich young ruler.* He calls Jesus, *'good' teacher* (Mark 10:17, Luke 18:18). Jesus doesn't respond by thanking him for the compliment, but instead rebukes him telling him to leave the word 'good' for God alone. Though Jesus didn't want to be labeled 'good', we spend our lives looking to label ourselves and have others call us 'good'.

When we have an image of our self or others, an image we define as 'good' or 'bad', the word 'should' often shows up. 'Good' parents should... 'Good' pastors should... 'Good' children should...

I came across a quote by Marshal Rosenberg, "Hell is the idea that there is such a thing as a 'good' parent." Not only is hell the idea there is such a thing as a 'good' parent, hell is also the idea there is such a thing as a good husband, a good wife, a good citizen, a good preacher, and, as in the previous story, a good samurai. How did the samurai create hell for himself with the idea of being a 'good' samurai? How do you create hell for yourself with the word 'good?'

Stepping Stone:
Let go of if/then lists.

With each image we label as 'good' or 'bad' comes a long *if _____ then _____* list.

In the story of the samurai, the samurai probably told himself, *if you are a good warrior, then people treat you with respect; if you are a good warrior, then people are afraid of you; if you are a good warrior, then people don't poor tea on you.*

What *if _____ then _____* lists do you have of yourself in the roles you play? For example, *if* I am a good parent, *then* my son will score goals in soccer. *If* my wife and I are good parents, *then* our children will never misbehave in public. *If* I am a good Christian, *then* I will never be frustrated with others. Think of images you have of yourself. What *if/then* lists have you created to go along with them.

Emptying yourself of your images, of your 'good' and 'bad' labels, dropping your *if _____ then _____* lists, will give you peace and allow you to have a connection with those you love in ways you have prevented yourself from in the past. It has for me. The best example is with my son. After I dropped the image of Good Dad rooted in my *if I'm a good dad, my son will excel in soccer,* I could actually see my son instead of just seeing how he reinforced or threatened my self image.

The Enlightenment of Jesus:

John 20: *Early on the first day of the week, while it was still dark, Mary Magdalene came to the tomb and saw that the stone had been removed from the tomb.* [2] *So she ran and went to Simon Peter and the other disciple, the one whom Jesus loved, and said to them, "They have taken the Lord out of the tomb, and we do not know where they have laid him."* [3] *Then Peter and the other disciple set out and went toward the tomb.* [4] *The two were running together, but the other disciple outran Peter and reached the tomb first.* [5] *He bent down to look in and saw the linen wrappings lying there, but he did not go in.* [6] *Then Simon Peter came, following him, and went into the tomb. He saw the linen wrappings lying there,* [7] *and the cloth that had been on Jesus' head, not lying with the linen wrappings but rolled up in a place by itself.* [8]

Then the other disciple, who reached the tomb first, also went in, and he saw and believed...

The disciples had many expectations, images of Jesus, images of who he should be as a 'good' Messiah. Those expectations of 'good' Messiahs kept them from seeing Easter. They also had images of 'good' followers which they had not met. Their expectations resulted in the disciples hiding and missing a miracle. Yet, Easter became a reality for them when they went to the empty place – the empty tomb, and saw the empty things – the empty grave clothes.

Easter begins in the empty place. For people tormented by images of good: good warriors, good parents, good teachers, good ministers, good citizens, life begins in emptiness. To enter nothing, to step into the void, is our holy journey. It is where, like the disciples, we encounter God. Meister Eckhart said,

It is characteristic of creatures that they make something out of something, while it is a characteristic of God that he makes something out of nothing. Therefore, if God is to make anything in you or with you, you must first become nothing. Hence go into your own ground and work there, and the works that you work there will all be living.

The first symbol of Easter is a void. Easter begins with nothing. Easter begins with the empty place. Easter begins with the empty tomb. And an invitation, "Come and see the empty place."

Emptiness opens us to possibility. As the proverb says, *It is not the bars but the space between them that holds the tiger.* Without space, there is no room for life symbolized by the tiger.

The priest in the samurai story used a cup as a symbol of self. Like the tea cup, it is not the pottery but it is the space between the pottery which gives life. Without space, the cup would be a ceramic ball – a poor ball that breaks soon after you throw it. It is the space that allows the cup its purpose. In a similar matter, not the notes but the empty space between them that creates the music. It is the empty places that make the music. In a similar manner, it is not the walls, but the space between them that makes a home... or a church. Without space, a church would be one giant block of concrete. Space makes room for life. We call church space between the walls 'sacred' space.

Easter invites us to let our minds be sacred space. The transformation of Easter, which took a tomb of death, and made it sacred, is to take your mind and make it sacred space – an empty place where you can experience the power of God to give full life.

What does God want from you? Nothing. And it may be one of the hardest things you have to give.

Epilogue:

Back at the soccer field, I watched as my son kicked the ball a couple of times, flew around like an airplane, a very happy airplane, then run from boy to boy trying to meet the players of the other team. I watched my son in awe that he could see a soccer game as a chance to meet new people, to get to know boys who might be his friends. While the others chased the ball, he ran around, "Hi, my name is Nathan..." "Hi, my name is Nathan..."

I thought about these two skills, scoring goals and meeting new people. I realized that for my son, the ability to meet new people and make new friends would likely serve him better in life than the ability to score soccer goals.

I still cheered for him, but I changed. "Go, Nathan! Run! You haven't met that boy over there, yet."

"Okay, Dad."

It worked for us, though his coach did look at me rather strangely, and I have not seen Jesus at Chuckie Cheese since.

Reflection:

Read the following quotes. How does each relate to the steps toward enlightenment described in this chapter?

God is not attained by a process of addition to anything in the soul, but by a process of subtraction.
Meister Eckhart

Meditation is not to escape from society, but to come back to ourselves and see what is going on. Once there is seeing, there must be acting. With mindfulness, we know what to do and what not to do to help.
Thich Nhat Hanh

Only in quiet waters do things mirror themselves undistorted.
Only in a quiet mind is adequate perception of the world.
Hans Margolius

as a flower blown out by the wind
goes to rest and cannot be defined
so the wise man freed from individuality
goes to rest and cannot be defined.
gone beyond all images-
gone beyond the power of words
Sutra Nipata

As my prayer became more attentive and inward,
I had less and less to say.
I finally became completely silent.
I started to listen
—which is even further removed from speaking.
I first thought that praying entailed speaking.
I then learnt that praying is hearing,
not merely being silent.
This is how it is.
To pray does not mean to listen to oneself speaking.
Prayer involves becoming silent,
and being silent,
and waiting until God is heard.
Soren Kierkegaard

Now what?

Fill out the chart below. On the left side write your roles.
Include job roles (boss, employee, student, etc.) and relationship roles
(parent, child, spouse, friend, etc.). Use another page if necessary.

If I am a good...	...then I will...
For example: Christian	Read my Bible, go to church, love my neighbor, never swear, etc...

Look back through your list...
    Which of those expectations have:
        been helpful to you in your relationships with others?
        been hurtful?
        made it easier for you to live with others?
        made it more difficult for you to live with others?
        made you easier to live with?
        made you harder to live with?

Go back through the list again. Circle the expectations you want
to keep of yourself and put a line through those you want to leave
behind. How will you change your thinking this week?

Encounter Six:
Images of the World

You have to ask children and birds
how cherries and strawberries taste.
Johann Wolfgang von Goethe

Flowers... notes tied to a fence... candles... parents standing in circles... several teddy bears... longing faces... empty chairs... empty desks... memorial portraits. I turned through the pages of the news magazine, read interviews with survivors, read a letter from the president, studied statistics about school shootings in America, and then I turned back through the magazine. This time, in place of the faces in pictures, I saw my children, children from my neighborhood, children from my congregation.

My heart's response was prayer. "Lord, please, help those students and families, and please, please, bring peace to the world, and bring it soon." At that moment, I noticed Jesus sitting beside me.

"You are pretty disappointed with me, aren't you?" he asked.

"What?" I asked surprised by his presence and his question. "Disappointed?"

"Yes," he said, "disappointed. You are disappointed in me."

I thought for a moment. "No," I said, "I'm not disappointed in you. Why would you..."

"Relax," Jesus said, "you are not the first person to be disappointed in me. People have always had images of me, and when I haven't lived up to them, they are disappointed. Don't you remember reading in the gospels, how disappointed my family was with me, how, after I healed a man, my mother and brothers came and tried to restrain me, they came to tell me to stop my ministry because their neighbors were saying that I was out of my mind.[3] Don't you remember how the man who was supposed to be my forerunner, John the Baptist, was disappointed in me? John called everybody out to the desert and said that the kingdom of God was coming; he pointed to me and said the kingdom of God was at

---

[3] (Mark 3:1-35, Matthew 12:46-50, and Luke 8:19-21)

hand.[4] He believed I would come and fix the world like he had been waiting for, hoping for, but I didn't. I didn't change the world at all. Then John was thrown in jail, in prison, waiting, hoping for fire from heaven, he became so frustrated with me that he sent his disciples to me with the question, 'Are you the one or should we look for someone else?' [5] Then there were my own disciples. Do you think Judas would have betrayed my location or Peter denied he knew me if they weren't disappointed in me? The most disappointed of all were the crowds in Jerusalem."

"The crowds?" I asked.

"Have you ever noticed how on my trip to Jerusalem, on Sunday they are shouting Hosannas and laying down Palm Branches, but by Thursday night the crowd has changed and is screaming, 'Crucify him!'?"

"Yes," I said.

"Would you like to know the reason?" Jesus asked.

"Yes," I said.

"Disappointment," Jesus said. "Everyone wanted me to give them peace by fixing the world. I refused. When I rode into Jerusalem, on a donkey, a symbol for a king coming in peace, they hoped I was bringing them peace by changing the world." Jesus paused for a moment. I could hear him breathe. He looked away from me and out the window. He turned back toward me and continued, "They were afraid. They were afraid of Rome, and they wanted Rome's destruction to end their fear. They were angry. They were angry at the priests, and they wanted the priests to be punished to appease their anger. They were ashamed, ashamed of their place in the world's hierarchy, and they wanted me to elevate them to a status of power which they hoped would relieve their shame. I refused. I refused it all. I didn't destroy Rome. I didn't punish the priests. I didn't elevate their status. So, when given a choice, when given a choice by Pilate, they chose Barabbas, a violent man who sought peace through ending the lives of enemies. That's the disappointment. I didn't fix the world."

I was silent.

---

[4] (Mark 1, Matthew 3, Luke 3, John 1)
[5] (Matthew 11:2-6, Luke 7:18-23)

"For two thousand years, people have prayed to me to destroy their enemies, to punish those who frustrate them, and to elevate them in the contemporary culture's hierarchy and much more. For two thousand years, people have prayed to me to make them safe, cure their aging bodies, give them a winning lottery ticket, and for two thousand years the result is that millions and millions of people have been very disappointed with me. More and more everyday."

Again I was quiet. I didn't know what to say. Could I say that I was disappointed in Jesus? I wasn't even sure I could think it. "I was praying for peace," I offered in an attempt to say something.

"Peace? Yes," he said. "You were praying for peace, but peace which could only come, in your way of thinking, if the world around you changed, if I changed the world. Your hope is that I will give you internal peace by changing your external world. You want me to fix those around you, fix your wife, kids, congregation, everybody because you believe that if the world around you gets *fixed* you'll have peace."

"Am I really like that? Do I really pray that way?" "Yes," he said. "Do you remember your frustration at the grocery store this morning?" Jesus asked.

I thought for a moment. I did. "But, Jesus, she was the slowest checker in all creation."

"So," Jesus said, "when you muttered, 'For the love of God, speed up!' wasn't that a prayer?"

I said nothing. What would you say? How would you respond?

Jesus continued, "Everyone prays, everyone cries out, everyone hopes, but most of their energy is focused on changing the world. What everyone who cries out in prayer wants is to have peace but what they ask for is for divine power to transform their situation. The goal is healthy, but the strategy is poor. Two thousand years, the world has changed little, yet, no one seems to notice. Humanity still seeks internal peace by fixing the world when the world neither has the potential for peace nor needs it. All that human energy focused outside of self while peace is only found on an internal journey. If the entire world was transformed into exactly what they wanted, they still wouldn't know peace. And," Jesus added... "you're no different."

Silence.

"No, probably not," I confessed.

Jesus continued, "I do want peace for the world, but it only begins within. Read the gospels. My purpose is clear. I sought to bring people peace so that through personal peace the world could be changed. Before there can be peace in the external world, people must find their peace within."

"Within?" I asked.

"You must have peace within before you can experience peace without..." Then he added, "Remember watching the report on the school shooting?"

"Yes," I said.

"What were you feeling?" Jesus asked.

"Sad, angry..."

"Anything else?"

"Afraid," I added.

"You've known about lots of murders of children from all over the world. This one stirred something in you. This one was personal. You identified with this one, didn't you?" he asked.

"Yes, I thought about my children and children that I know," I admitted.

"Right," Jesus said. "This one was different from others in what you felt. Pay attention to what's going on inside of you..."

Apparently Jesus had said all he had to say, for I looked next to me and he was gone.

Movement:
From expectations of the world as it isn't
to acceptance of the world as it is.

Stepping Stone:
Step into reality by stepping out of your illusions.

Much of our pain comes from illusions, images we create for ourselves. My torment in reading the news magazine came from the image of my children being shot. The shooting was real, the image of my children and children I cared about was not. The imagined tragedy was what tormented me most.

To deal with the real world, we have to first step out of the world of our illusions, our imagination, our nightmares. There is a Buddhist story of demons which can help us step out of our self created nightmares.

Long ago, in Tibet, there was a ceremony, held every hundred years, which Buddhist students could undergo in order to attain enlightenment. All the students would line up in their white robes. The lamas – the Tibetan priests – and the Dalai Lama would line up before the students. The Dalai Lama would begin the ceremony by saying, "This is the ceremony of the Room of 1000 Demons. It is a ceremony for enlightenment, and it happens only once every hundred years. If you choose not to go through it now, you will have to wait another hundred years. To help you make this decision, we'll tell you what the ceremony involves.

"In order to enter the Room of 1000 Demons, you just open the door and walk in. The Room of 1000 Demons is not very big. Once you enter, the door will close behind you. There is no doorknob on the inside of the door. In order to get out, you will have to walk all the way through the room, find the door on the other side, open the door, which is unlocked, and come out. Then you will be enlightened.

"The room is called the Room of 1000 Demons because there are one thousand demons in there. Those demons have the ability to take on the form of your worst fears... As soon as you walk into the room, those demons show you your worst fears. If you have a fear of heights, when you walk into the room it will appear as if you are standing on a narrow ledge of a tall building. If you have a fear of spiders, you'll be surrounded by the most

terrifying eight-legged creatures imaginable. *Whatever your fears are, the demons take those images from your mind and seem to make them real. In fact, they'll be so compellingly real that it will be very difficult to remember that they're not.*

"*We can't come in and rescue you. That is part of the rules. If you go into the Room of 1000 Demons, you must leave it on your own...*

"*If you want to enter the room, we have two hints for you. The first hint: As soon as you enter the Room of 1000 Demons, remember that what they show you isn't real. It's all from your own mind. Don't buy into it; it's an illusion... The second hint has been more helpful for the people who made it out the other side and became enlightened. Once you go into the room, no matter what you see, no matter what you feel, no matter what you hear, no matter what you think, keep your feet moving. If you keep your feet moving, you will eventually get to the other side, find the door, and come out.*"[6]

Do you have a room of 1,000 demons? Can you step out of it?

Stepping Stone:
See the futility of your efforts
to gain peace through useless wishing.

I have a propensity toward trying to give myself peace by changing the world, often in some strange ways. Like this one...

Early one morning, our house had contained sleeping parents and children, until a horn woke us up. Apparently, someone was getting picked up next door, but instead of going to the door, the driver just sat in the car and blew his horn...then again...then again.

I thought to myself, 'I want to be Gandalf (the wizard from Tolkien's *The Lord of the Rings*).' I waved my hands in small circles and hummed. I imagined myself magically causing the tires on the car next door to explode.

"What are you doing?" Carrie asked me.

"I am magically causing all the tires on their car to go flat," I said.

"Oh," she said.

The horn blew twice next door. I waved my hand again.

---

[6] *Bill O'Hanlon (1999) Do One Thing Different: Ten Simple Ways to Change Your Life.*

"What now?" she asked.

"I'm magically causing their horn to go mute," I said.

HONK!

I swayed my whole body from side to side.

"What are you doing now?" Carrie asked.

"I'm causing the car to catch on fire so that the driver will run away, and all will be quiet," I said.

"How's that working for you?" she asked.

I then began waving my hands at her. "Shhhh," I said.

I often catch myself wanting power to control the world, to end all my frustrations by magically, prayerfully, hopefully changing current reality to calm my rage within, yet, with little results.

The ancient advice serves me well, "Don't just see the tree, but see yourself seeing the tree." When I see myself and not just my circumstances, I can see how futile my efforts to finding peace by wishing change upon the world can be. Only then do I choose to let go of those efforts and search for the key to my frustration within.

Watch what frustrates you this week. See what you focus on, yourself or the frustration.

Stepping Stone:
See the pain you cause yourself
by trying to change others.

I remember a man who came to me irritated about his ex-wife. "There is something really wrong with her," he said.

"She is mentally off," I agreed but added, "as are we all. I find the one thing we all have in common is that we are all mentally ill to some degree." He did not see the humor or wisdom. I remained quiet.

For the rest of the hour, I listened and said little; he said much. He complained about his world and the people in it, specifically his ex-wife. His premise was clear, "I have no peace. If only she would change, then I would be fine." During his rant, I must have said something, but none of it was memorable. I thought back to my training in seminary. My professor said, "As a pastor, people will come to you for counseling. They are looking to you for advice, guidance and direction, with one caveat: that they don't have to change. What they want to know is simply this, 'How can I keep doing exactly what I've always done and get different results.'" "Isn't that the definition of insanity?" we asked. "Exactly," he responded. "They want all your counsel to help them change the world around them."

I listened to the man, "How can I get her to change?" He asked me.

With an opportunity to speak given, I wanted to offer advice, instead all I did was ask a question hoping the advice would be evident, "How did you get her to change before the divorce?"

"Oh, I never could get her to change before the divorce. That's one of the main reasons we got divorced."

"Well," I said, "if you couldn't get her to change before the divorce, then its unlikely you'll get her to change now."

He looked at me as if he had just asked marital advice from a three year old. I just smiled. He did not smile back. His look of disgust said it all. He was disappointed with me. I hadn't changed his world.

Whether it is changing an individual or the world as a whole, those efforts seldom show much positive affect.

Who have you been trying to change to give yourself peace of mind? Do you think you'll do any better changing them in the future than you have thus far?

Stepping Stone:
Look for peace by searching within.

Whatever your dissatisfaction, aggravation, or frustration, the key to your personal peace is not outside of you but within you. Searching for your key to peace outside yourself will only add to your frustration and the frustration of others who live with you as shown through this next story...

A group of students came upon their teacher outside his home. He was looking through the bushes and in the grass of his yard.

"What are you looking for?" the students asked.

"Oh," he said seeming surprised to see them. "I am looking for the key to my house."

"We will help you," his students replied.

After about an hour of searching, one of the students asked, "Where did you lose your key?"

The teacher pointed to his home, "I lost the key inside my house."

All the students looked up at the teacher as the first one asked, "Then why are you looking out here?"

"The light is better out here," the teacher laughed and walked back inside his house.

How can you start looking within for peace?

Stepping Stone:
Claim your power. Claim your peace.

Anthony De Mello in *Awareness* wrote of how illusions can cause pain:

Anytime you have a negative feeling toward anyone, you're living in an illusion. There's something seriously wrong with you. You're not seeing reality. Something inside of you has to change. But what do we generally do when we have a negative feeling? "He is to blame, she is to blame. She's got to change" No! The world's all right. The one who has to change is you.[7]

According to De Mello, the Bible begins with an affirmation, "The world is all right." In the first chapter of Genesis, when God creates the world, God calls the world, "Good." God's declaration of 'good' for the world doesn't mean perfect, flawless, without challenge, chaos free, or pure but all right, okay, satisfactory and satisfying. So, for us to live at peace in the world, we must accept the world as is.

If there is something we want to have different in the world, altering the world we live in begins by accepting it as is. Then you can be present. To be present in the world as is takes overcoming the barriers within. De Mello gives some simple steps toward living in the world.

The first thing *you need to do is get in touch with negative feelings that you're not even aware of. Lots of people have negative feelings they're not*

---

[7] Pg. 51

aware of. Lots of people are depressed and they're not aware they are depressed. It's only when they make contact with joy that they understand how depressed they were...

The second step...is to understand that the feeling is in you, not in reality... Negative feelings are in you, not in reality. So stop trying to change reality. That's crazy! Stop trying to change the other person. We spend all our time and energy trying to change external circumstances, trying to change our spouses, our bosses, our friends, our enemies, and everybody else. We don't have to change anything. Negative feelings are in you. No person on earth has the power to make you unhappy. There is no event on earth that has the power to disturb you or hurt you. No event, condition, situation, or person...

The Enlightenment of Jesus:

Jesus offers an alternative to 'looking for the world to change to give me peace' mentality. He offers an alternative to the mind of 1,000 demons, and he does so in Mark 10:[13] *People were bringing little children to (Jesus) in order that he might touch them; and the disciples spoke sternly to them.* [14] *But when Jesus saw this, he was indignant and said to them, "Let the little children come to me; do not stop them; for it is to such as these that the kingdom of God belongs.* [15] *Truly I tell you, whoever does not receive the kingdom of God as a little child will never enter it."* [16] *And he took them up in his arms, laid his hands on them, and blessed them.*

Instead of the room of 1,000 Demons, Jesus offers the kingdom of God. The prerequisite is the mind of a child. Whereas adults must experience the kingdom to see the kingdom, children experience the kingdom because they see the kingdom. To become like a child is to take on child like vision and experience the kingdom because we see the kingdom. My children teach me often.

One of the best lessons I have gotten was from my eldest daughter, Cayla, who taught me to appreciate trash trucks.

Before Cayla, I hated trash trucks because trash trucks come early in the morning. My attitude was shaped in my college days at Clemson, when, while sleeping in the dorm, the trash truck would come with the sunrise, pick up the huge metal containers, bang them loudly, crash them down and then back up. Backing up was the worst because of that hideous "beep beep beep" when the truck went in reverse. I could not get the pillow tight enough around my head.

For years, long after college, when the trash truck would come into our neighborhood, I would curse it under my breath. I would snarl, "Trash truck!" But not with Cayla. She showed me a better way. She converted me. She showed me the beauty of trash truck love.

I began to love the trash truck when Cayla was around two years old, because she loved the trash truck. She would hear the trash truck in the morning, and, if she was already awake, she would shout, "Trash truck! Trash truck!" and run for the window to watch the men take our garbage cans.

If asleep when the truck rolled into our neighborhood, Cayla would wake up and shout, "Daddy, trash truck!" She would wait for me to run upstairs, grab her from the bed, and carry her to the window. "Daddy, trash truck," she would say.

My experience changed because my perception changed. I caught her enthusiasm. I too shouted "Trash truck! Trash truck!" If I would hear the truck coming, I would go and wake her up. I would say, "Cayla," and she would hardly move (to this day not an early riser without cause). I would whisper, "Trash truck" and she would sit up, reach out her arms to me, hold on tight, and we would run to the window.

The excitement of "Trash truck! Trash truck!" made once ordinary Thursday mornings become Terrific Thursdays. The enthusiasm didn't just fill one day a week. No, it began with a Christmas-like anticipation the night before as we gathered the trash and took it to the roadside knowing that the trash truck would come in the morning. In equal excitement to the potential arrival of St. Nick, Cayla would say, "Daddy, trash truck is coming to take my diapers."

The kingdom of heaven belongs to such as her. She has been a great teacher for me. So often now do I try and experience the kingdom of heaven through this simple skill I learned from my children – you want to experience the kingdom? Then see the kingdom...first.

Reflection:

Read the following quotes. How does each relate to the steps toward enlightenment described in this chapter?

All God wants of man is a peaceful heart.
Meister Eckhart

There are two great disappointments in life:
not getting what you want,
and getting it.
George Bernard Shaw

Your vision will become clear
only when you look into your heart ...
Who looks outside, dreams.
Who looks inside, awakens.
Carl Jung

If you understand, things are just as they are;
if you do not understand, things are just as they are.
Zen Proverb

Everyone thinks of changing the world,
but no one thinks of changing himself.
Leo Tolstoy

See if you can catch yourself complaining in either speech or thought, about a
situation you find yourself in, what other people do or say, your surroundings,
your life situation, even the weather.
To complain is always nonacceptance of what is. It invariably carries an
unconscious negative charge. When you complain, you make yourself a
victim. Leave the situation or accept it. All else is madness.
Eckart Tolle

Now what?

Fill in the chart below: On the left side write a person or thing you want to change. Think of people who are important to you, but also think broader, including neighbors, community, the nation, the world.

What I want to change:	What I want changed:
For example, spouse	Snores at night. Won't lower the lid. Talks to mom on the phone too long. etc.

After you finish your lists, go back through and cross out each item under *What I want changed* that you don't think is likely to change much if at all.

How can you commit yourself to spending less energy on what you can't change and more energy on what you can change – including your perspective?

End with The Serenity Prayer. *God grant me the serenity to accept the things I cannot change; the courage to change the things I can; and most of all, grant me the wisdom to know the difference.*

Encounter Seven:
Images of Life

Can you drink the cup?
Can you empty it to the dregs?
Can you taste all the sorrows and joys?
Can you live your life to the full whatever it will bring?
Henri Nouwen

The next visit I had with Jesus was before a wedding. I was in the typical pastoral holding pattern. I had opened up the church, checked with bride and groom, put the bulletins out, and final proofed my written remarks. All in motion, I soared about the church with nothing to do.

Just because I was circling didn't mean I wasn't nervous. Weddings and funerals stir anxiety in me. In weddings, like funerals, you don't get a 'do over.' On a weekly Sunday service, if, as worship leader, you don't have your 'best stuff', if the sermon is off or you stumble over the liturgy, it's okay because the next Sunday you get to do it all again – a 'do over.' However, if you botch a wedding, they won't put it all together again for you the next weekend any more than a family would sit through another funeral just because no one recognized the person you spoke of in your eulogy.

On this particular Saturday wedding holding pattern, I perceived that my wits were a little hazy. My unusually large lunch geared my mind more toward napping than nuptials. For a little pick-me up, I went down to the church kitchen to put on a pot of coffee. Our church has a two-tier coffee maker with two burners on top to keep a couple of pots warm, and below is a single burner for the pot which catches the coffee.

I, in my mental thinking-about-the-service fog, filled the filter and hit start. Then, and only then, did I notice there was no pot on the lower tier. The coffee was flowing out of the filter onto the burner. Fortunately, there was a pot on top. I assumed a clean, empty pot. I assumed incorrectly. The pot on top was half full. It had been left from the previous Wednesday night dinner. As soon as I jerked it from its spot, cold, old coffee shot into the air and came down all over my coat, tie, and previously white shirt.

After saying several words only allowed to liberal preachers, I looked up to the ceiling in prayer and said, "Why me?"

Then he spoke.

Jesus was sitting on the counter next to me. "Why not you?" he asked.

"What do you mean?" I barked back. "I have old coffee all over my white shirt and in a half hour I'm going to be doing a wedding."

"Yes," Jesus said, "I know all of that, but why not you?"

I said nothing. I just cursed under my breath.

"Why not you?" Jesus asked again. "You know the saying, 'What goes up must come down.' Why shouldn't it come down on you?"

The brain steam escaped through my mouth, "Because a lot of money, energy and time went into this day for the couple. They are expecting a less soiled pastor to preside."

"Yes," Jesus said again, "but why not you? Why shouldn't the coffee land on you?"

"Because," I said, "I am officiating the wedding, a special cause, a special purpose in which I have a special sacred role. I am the only one here who can marry them. That's why I shouldn't get coffee dumped on me."

"Dumped on you?" Jesus asked. "So you think it was dumped on you? Is God out to get you or have you personified gravity?"

"Fall on me," I restated. "I am here for a special, sacred, holy purpose, that's why I shouldn't have coffee fall on me. Because I am doing what I'm called to do. I am serving as I am asked to serve. I am being faithful to my duties to the congregation. That's why."

"So," Jesus laughed, "let me get this straight. The special nature of the day, your specific role, and your faithfulness should give you an exemption from mishaps. This special nature of your role on this special day should make you immune from silly," and at that looked at me and laughed again, "and I do mean silly, accidents."

At that point I felt liquid on my cheek. I had a nice stream coming down from my hair. I was certain it was brown and caffeinated. "Well, since you put it that way... "I thought for a moment. I've never been one to give in easily on a debate, but by this point I had added anger to frustration. "Yes!" I exclaimed. "Yes, I want an exemption. I would like a break from this annoying stuff, these silly accidents that ruin my day, that frustrate me, keep me from my work. Yes, I want an exemption."

"There you are," Jesus said, "sleeping again. You have an image of the world far removed from reality. In your image of the world, there are exemptions for faithful people especially on special days when they are doing *good* things. In this image of the world you have, it's not supposed to rain on birthdays, weddings, funerals, church picnics, soccer games, or any other special days. Car tires should be immune to flats when operating on church business. Church copier machines should never jam when doing the bulletin. Ministers should never have coffee spill on them. Should I keep going?"

"No," I said wiping the coffee from my face. "I think you've got it."

"You, my friend," Jesus said, "are not only sleeping through life, you are sleeping through church."

"Sleeping through church," I said indignantly, "what do you mean? I'm the pastor. I don't sleep through church, I put people to sleep."

"I know you are the pastor," Jesus said, "which makes your sleeping all the more impressive. Forget the famous proverb I quote 'it rains on the just and the unjust alike,' if you were awake, you might read it 'coffee falls on the just and unjust alike,' but because you are mostly asleep, in your vision of the world, the just don't have to worry about rain or coffee. Forget that passage, you could easily over look it, but you should have noticed the cross. You stand in front of it each week. How have you not thought about the cross?"

"What do you mean?" I asked.

"How many of your images of me have titles?" Jesus asked.

"Lots," I said.

"What are some of my titles you can think of?" Jesus asked.

"Son of Man, Son of God, Immanuel, Christ, Messiah, Lion of Judah, Lamb of God, God's Chosen..." I said.

"Right," Jesus said, "in your mind, you connect me with all of those images and the titles that go with them, yet, you ignore the implication of the cross. Don't you find it odd that in your image of the world, the Son of Man, Son of God, Immanuel, Christ, Messiah, Lion of Judah, Lamb of God, God's Chosen, can go to the cross, yet, the pastor about to officiate a wedding shouldn't have coffee dumped on him? If, when it came to the cross, 'why not me' then when it comes to coffee, 'why not you?'"

I have officiated funeral services for children, for youth, for people I cared about who, in my judgment, died too young, yet, still in my mind, I was holding tightly to an image of the world where I shouldn't get coffee landing on me - on special days particularly.

"Okay," I said. "So maybe my images of the world and my life in it have some intense self observation work to do."

"Now you are actually talking like a person awake!" Jesus said. "Think about all these things. Start noticing the images you have of the world, and the expectations you have that go with them, but don't start now. Start later, because now you've got a *special* job to do..."

"Special job?" I asked.

Jesus didn't say anything. I looked to see him pointing his finger at my now tan shirt.

"I've got to change my clothes! I've got a wedding!" I shouted.

Jesus was gone.

Movement:
From expectations of life
which bring disappointment
to acceptance of life
which brings peace.

Stepping Stone:
Accept the fragile nature of humanity.

We die.

All of us.

Jesus died. Moses died. Mother Teresa died. You'll die. I'll die. By the time you are reading this book, I may be dead already.

My intention is not to overstate the obvious, but our mortality needs reminders. We like to forget it.

I have generally been well received as a speaker at youth events (at least I like to think so). There was one occasion when I was well received by the youth, but not the youth leaders.

I was asked to speak at an event in Columbia, South Carolina. I had told them I would be glad to come if I could pick the theme. They said, "Sure." Then I got a call, "The youth didn't like any of your themes. They picked their own. They want the theme of the weekend to be 'I will survive.'"

"I will survive?" I asked. "Where did they come up with the theme?"

"From that song from the 70's," was the reply.

"Great," I said.

The problem with not letting me pick a theme is that you may choose one I don't believe. I've seen too much. I know the deception of a theme like "I will survive," no matter how popular the song may have been.

I started the weekend on stage, in front of all the youth, by saying, "Our theme is 'I will survive'. Let me hear you shout, 'I will survive!'"

Over and over I had them shout, "I will survive! I will survive! I will survive!"

Then I asked, "How do you know?"

Silence.

I waited. I let the question spread across the room like the smell of popcorn from a microwave. Then I said, "You don't. You don't know if you will survive or not. There are no guarantees. I want to talk about your mortality, and your faith."

That was where we began.

They never asked me back to speak.

Stepping Stone:

Accept your mortality.

We deny our certain death, similar to the woman in this story...

A woman went to see her doctor to get the results of her medical tests. The doctor responded. "I'm sorry to tell you that it doesn't look good."

"Really?" she asked quite concerned. "Is it fatal?"

"Yes, I'm afraid so," the doctor responded.

"How much time to I have left?" she asked.

"Ten," the doctor replied.

"Ten?" she asked. "Ten what? Years? Months? Weeks?"

"Nine...," he said. "Eight... Seven..."

She understood that she could die, then found out a lot sooner than she thought.

Ernest Becker said that much of our time alive is wasted in denying our mortality. Becker observed:

1. We die.

2. We don't like it.

3. We spend much of our energy, and thus much of our lives, avoiding the fact that we die.

To awaken to life, we must first accept our mortality.

Do you agree with Ernest Becker that people generally spend a lot of their life's energy avoiding the reality of our death? Why or why not?

In what ways do you see yourself spending much of your life's energy denying your mortality?

Stepping Stone:
Accept the reality of problems.

Buddha said, "Life is suffering." He did not think this was bad news, but a statement of reality intended to free the hearer from expecting otherwise as shown in this story...

There once was a man who had some problems. He went to the Buddha to see if he might be able to help him out. He told the Buddha about his farm. "I like farming," he said, "but sometimes it doesn't rain enough, and my crops fail, and we starve. Sometimes it rains too much, so my crops aren't what I want them to be."

The Buddha did not say anything.

The man continued, "I'm married. She's a good wife. I love her. But sometimes she nags me. Sometimes I get tired of her."

The Buddha did not say anything.

The man continued, "I have kids. Good kids, but sometimes they don't show me enough respect."

The Buddha did not say anything. The man continued in several other areas of his life. He waited for the Buddha to speak and say something to make his life better, to put everything right, but the Buddha didn't say anything. "Well," said the man. "Can you help me?"

The Buddha said, "I can't help you ...Everybody's got problems... In fact, we've all got eighty-three problems, and there's nothing you can do about it. If you work really hard on one of them, maybe you can fix it – but if you do another one will pop right into its place..."

The man became furious. "I thought you were a great Buddha!" he shouted. "I thought you could help me! What good are you if you can't help me by fixing my world?"

The Buddha replied, "Maybe I can help you. Now, you are a lot like everyone else. Everyone else, like you, has eighty-three problems. But you, you have eighty-four problems. I think I can help you with your eighty-fourth problem."

"You can?" the man asked. "What is my eighty-fourth problem?"

"Your extra problem is that you think you're not supposed to have any problems."

Make a list of problems you are facing this week. Are there any on your list you think you shouldn't have?

Stepping Stone:
Claim your power to choose your response
no matter what the circumstances.

Though we cannot choose our circumstances (whether a pot of cold, or hot, coffee falls on us, whether or not a meteor from outer space lands on our children's trampoline, or the check out clerk at the grocery store is mean to us) we can choose our response. Though we cannot choose how life or other people treat us, we can choose how we act. Notice I didn't say *react* but *act*. *React* denies our power to choose. Here is one of the great stories of choice in the midst of horrible circumstances...

In a concentration camp lived a prisoner. Even though he was under the sentence of execution, this prisoner was boundless and free. One day he was seen in the middle of the prison playing his guitar. A large crowd gathered to listen to the music. They all joined in song, and for a moment, felt as free as he. When the guards saw this, they ordered the crowd to disperse and the man to never play his guitar again.

The next day, he was back singing and playing on his guitar, but this time he had an even larger crowd. The guards took him away and had his fingers chopped off.

The next day he was back, singing and making what music he could with his bleeding fingers. This time the crowds were cheering. The guards dragged him away again and smashed his guitar.

The following day he was singing with all his heart. The crowd joined in, and while the singing lasted, their hearts became as free as his. So angry were the guards this time that they had his tongue torn out. The concentration camp was silent. They were sure the minstrel was defeated.

The next day he was out in the middle of the concentration camp dancing and swaying to a silent music in his head. The crowd gathered around him and held hands. Soon everyone was dancing around this bleeding broken figure while the guards did the only thing they could do, look on in wonder.

How can you choose to make music in the midst of your struggles?

Stepping Stone:
No matter what the storm,
let go of things beyond your control.

Horatio Spafford was a successful businessman in Chicago. The fire in 1871 which wiped out much of Chicago took a lot of his wealth. He helped rebuild the city and worked with many who were left homeless in the disaster. A couple of years later, he arranged for him and his family to go on a vacation to Europe. At the last minute, business kept him in Chicago, but he sent his family on ahead. The ship his family was traveling on was hit by another boat. Only a fifth of the crew survived. His wife alone of his family survived. Their four daughters died.

When she reached Europe, she cabled back, "Saved alone. What shall I do?"

Horatio immediately started for Europe. On the way, the captain pointed out the place where he believed Horatio's daughters had died. Horatio returned to his cabin, and began writing the hymn, "It is Well."

When peace, like a river, attendeth my way,
when sorrows like sea billows roll;
whatever my lot, thou hast taught me to say,
It is well, it is well with my soul.

The Enlightenment of Jesus:

John 16:33 *"I have told you these things, so that in me you may have peace. In this world you will have trouble. But take heart! I have overcome the world."* (NIV)

Like Buddha, Jesus tells his hearers that in this world there are troubles. This isn't to be a surprise, but instead good news. Once we accept this life has problems, we can turn away from denial of life's difficulties and accept them. In acceptance, we find peace. Jesus also said, John 14: [27] *Peace I leave with you; my peace I give to you. I do not give to you as the world gives. Do not let your hearts be troubled, and do not let them be afraid.* Jesus' faith didn't give him a life free from pain. When he said this to his followers, he was headed toward the cross. Though

I'm confident you won't be nailed to a cross, I am also confident you will have your struggles, ranging from potential coffee stains to concentration camps; how you will respond will shape your experience and possibly the world. It begins with you, and with your expectations. Do you expect troubles? Do Jesus' words 'in this world you will have troubles' sound like good news to you?

Reflection:

Read the following quotes. How does each relate to the steps toward enlightenment described in this chapter?

> We understand why children are afraid of darkness,
> but why are men afraid of light?
> Plato

> Whereas the average individuals "often have not the slightest idea of what they are, of what they want, of what their own opinions are," self-actualizing individuals have "superior awareness of their own impulses, desires, opinions, and subjective reactions in general."
> Abraham Maslow

> I saw grief drinking a cup of sorrow and called out, "it tastes sweet, does it not?" "You've caught me," grief answered, "and you've ruined my business, how can I sell sorrow when you know it's a blessing?"
> Rumi

> Suffering is the sandpaper of our life.
> It does its work of shaping us.
> Suffering is part of our training program for becoming wise.
> Ram Dass

> Joy is a mystery because it can happen anywhere, anytime,
> even under the most unpromising circumstances,
> even in the midst of suffering, with tears in its eyes.
> Frederich Buechner

Now what?

Think of problems you want to let go in your life, problems you've been holding onto tightly. Write them down here.

Beside the problem you want to let go, write down what you want instead. Perhaps you want to let go of frustration you have with a coworker. What you want instead is a joy you once had at your job.

Pray the palms down/palms up prayer. While sitting, with your palms down on your knees, pray, "God, I let go of (and name what you want to let go of)." Then, turn your palms over in a receiving stance, and pray, "God, I ask you for (and name what you want instead)." For example, "(Palms down) God, I let go of my fear, and (palms up) I ask you for your peace."

How can you claim what you asked for this week through your actions?

Encounter Eight:
Attachment

The tighter you squeeze, the less you have.
Zen Proverb

Day One

As a parent, I always secretly wanted my children's first word to be, "Daddy." "Dad" is a wonderful word. "Dad" is used in homecomings, "Dad is home." In joyous celebrations, "Dad, watch this!" On the other hand, "Mom" is used when children want something. "Mom! I can't find my shoes."

Yet, no matter how much I wanted for my eldest child's first utterance to be, "Dad," no matter how often I pointed to myself and said, "Da, Da, Da, Dad," her first word was, "Pooh." Pooh, our chocolate lab, was a year old when Cayla was born. Before Cayla came home from the hospital, I brought her cap into the house, full of Cayla's aroma, and let Pooh know she could smell it but not touch. As a tiny baby, held in our arms, Cayla would watch the lab's movements through the house. When vanished from site, Cayla would look around, and as soon as able, ask, "Pooh?" "Pooh?"

As a toddler, on more than one occasion, Cayla walked through the house, got tired and sat down, on Pooh's head. I still remember the look on Pooh's face as she peered from under the diapered bottom and bootied feet of my daughter. The look was an easy translation, "How much longer do I have to put up with this?" Yet, faithful and true, she did not move, growl or show any discomfort other than what her eyes declared.

At some point in her training, I must have used a rolled up magazine to teach Pooh not to poo on the carpet. One day, when playing with two year old Cayla, I tapped a rolled up magazine on the floor and said to Cayla teasing, "I'm going to get you." Though Cayla giggled as I chased her, Pooh still perceived the magazine as a threat to Cayla. Pooh ran across the room and bit the magazine from my hand. Cayla and I looked at each other in amazement. "Cool!"

We trained Pooh to sit and stay. Cayla would lie upon the floor. I would pretend to hit her with the magazine. Pooh would come running and jump over Cayla taking the magazine from my hand. Anytime people came over, Cayla or I would say, "We have a trick to show you." We especially enjoyed scaring guests who weren't dog people. Typically, as Pooh leapt over Cayla, the guests would shriek, and we would laugh.

One of my favorite pictures is of Cayla, at one of her first snows, outside trying to catch snow flakes with her tongue while Pooh licked them from her face.

All these memories flooded my mind while I held Pooh's face in my hands and she died. We were at the vet's office. Pooh, then thirteen, had numerous tumors including one on the bottom of her foot, severe hip displasia, and was losing control of her nervous system. After she panted her last breath, the vet left me alone in the room with her body. That's when Jesus appeared. He said nothing. He simply stood by me as I cried my goodbye.

I took a deep breath, gathered myself, I turned to leave the room. Jesus had gone.

Day Two

In the evening, I sat out on our deck looking over the back yard where Pooh spent much of her time. Jesus appeared again, sitting beside me.

"She was a first-rate dog," I said.

"Faithful and devoted," Jesus said.

We looked out at the yard. A breeze caused the swings to sway. "Are you here to teach me something?" I asked.

"When you are ready," he said.

"I guess I'm ready. After all, every experience is an opportunity to learn more about the book of me," I said.

He laughed a soft laugh, looked at me and smiled.

"The pain you felt yesterday, at the veterinarian's office, when Pooh died..."

"Yes?"

"I want to give that pain a name," he said.

"Okay," I offered.

"Attachment," he said. "Attachment is the connection you felt with Pooh and your thoughts about Pooh. Attachment is the source of the pain. Because you were attached to Pooh in your mind, at her loss, you experienced significant pain."

I felt a little anger, "Do you mean I shouldn't feel attached to my dog, or to anyone or anything else?"

"No," Jesus said. "What I am saying..."

I interrupted. "How can we live without feeling attachment? How can you love without feeling attached? How could I have a pet for thirteen years and not feel attached. Am I supposed to believe that attachment is bad?"

"Peace," he said. "Be still. Relax. Breathe deep and listen. First, in our time together of instruction, lose the words 'should,' 'good,' and 'bad.' They are not helpful but actually prevent you from seeing. Whatever is present in you is worth examining without evaluating. Whatever is the root of your experience is worth noting without judgment. At Pooh's passing, you felt pain. With some observation, you can see that the pain comes from a sense of attachment. I'm not scolding you for your attachment. I am inviting you to look into yourself and see your attachments."

"Okay," I said, much calmer. "Sorry."

"Like 'should,' 'good,' and 'bad,' 'sorry' has little use here. You felt angry because I touched a very sore place for you, a place of pain. Don't apologize for the pain. See it. Understand it."

"Attachment," I said.

"Clearly, because of the pain at your loss, you were attached to Pooh. You have many attachments. Let's look at some of the signs of attachment. Consider yesterday, when you couldn't find your keys and your mobile phone, how did you feel?"

"I felt lost without them. I wasn't sure I could function without my keys and my phone," I replied.

"Feeling lost is a sign of attachment. If you feel you are incomplete without certain objects, then you are attached. What about the day before yesterday, when Carrie was painting the bonus room, do you remember being angry?"

"Yes, of course I do, she got paint on my favorite Clemson sweatshirt. I wore that sweatshirt in college. I wore it to multiple football games. They were ten and two when I wore that shirt. That shirt is a family heirloom I planned to pass on to Nathan when he was old enough, provided it doesn't get too many more holes. A priceless treasure and she got paint on it!"

"To not respect the shirt was to not respect you?" Jesus asked.

"Yes. How could she not think about how important that sweatshirt is to me?" I asked.

"Disrespect is another sign of attachment. When disrespect to an object is perceived as disrespect to self, when taking an object lightly is considered as taking you lightly, then clearly there is attachment with the object. Can you think of another emotion that might surface if someone identifies or is attached to an object?"

"Fear?" I asked.

"Sure," Jesus said. "Anytime someone is attached to an object, they fear losing it."

"But I lost a close friend in my dog," I said. "She was not an object."

"People are attached to more than objects. People attach self to pets, people, as well as ideas, images, thoughts and beliefs. Attachment results from identification. Anything you identify with can result in attachment. Something doesn't have to be tangible to associate self with it. Consider your images of self. You are attached to several because you identify who you are through your images. Remember Preacher Guy and how hard you worked to justify the image that you are a good preacher by trying to write a sermon which people would leave Easter Sunday and go call a friend to tell them about it? You identify self with that image, especially at Easter. Remember Nathan's soccer game and you wanted him to score a goal to justify your image of self as a Good Parent?"

"Are those identifications bad? Shouldn't I want to be a good parent and a good preacher?"

"Again, lose the should, good, and bad labeling. Just see. If you can look at yourself, seeing your identifications, then you can see the consequences. By identifying with the image of Good Preacher you had a difficult time seeing the new family that joined the church. All you saw was how they reinforced your idea of self by telling you they thought you were the best preacher they had heard. As Good Parent you were blind to the happiness of your son because you only saw his lack of intensity at soccer you thought the son of a good parent should have. Identifications close and blind, they alienate and separate."

"What about beliefs? You said we can identify with and attach ourselves to beliefs."

"Beliefs, values, opinions, even attitudes," Jesus said. "You don't need anything as strong as a belief to identify with and attach self to it. Something as small as an opinion or attitude is all it takes for most people to attach self to their thoughts."

"Am I most people?" I asked.

"Remember the argument you had yesterday with your neighbor about the president?"

"Yes," I replied.

"The two of you were ready to come to blows because each identified with his ideas about the president and government. Neither of you actually saw or heard the other through the identifications."

"So I identify with Pooh? That's where the pain has come from, my identification?" I asked.

"In a similar fashion, you identified with ideas about her, who you imaged she is, who you remember she was."

"What do you mean?" I asked.

"Most identification comes from some association with the past. Your Clemson shirt connects you to a stage of life that is long past. You haven't let go of yesterday, thus you cling to the ragged sweatshirt. If you would have let go of yesterday, if you were no longer associating yourself with your past, with who you used to be, the Clemson shirt would mean little to you."

"Oh, no," I said. "Don't tell me that Twenty Year Old Guy is showing up again!"

"Sort of," Jesus said. "Just recognize that your attachment to the Clemson shirt is as much an attachment to the past as it is to the shirt."

"Okay," I said. "But what does this have to do with Pooh?"

"You identify with Pooh, but not just Pooh. You also identify strongly with your images of who she used to be. In many ways you identify more with who she used to be five years ago than who she was when she died," Jesus said.

"I don't understand."

"Every time you felt tears coming on during Pooh's death, what were you thinking about?"

"Fond memories of our family with Pooh," I said.

"How recent were the memories?" Jesus asked.

I thought through my mental scrap book of Pooh. All of my fond memories were back over four years ago, before Pooh's hips and walking got severely impaired. "A while back," I said.

"Yes," said Jesus. "You haven't let go of your identification with the younger Pooh. Of late, you have hardly seen Pooh at all. Who has taken care of Pooh these last couple of years more, you or Carrie?"

"Carrie," I said.

"Yes," said Jesus. "You distanced yourself from her as her health worsened. You identified with the past and couldn't see her because you never let go of your images of who she used to be. Her aging health was contrary to your image of her. As a result, you kept your distance. During her death, not only was she dying, but so were the images of her as a puppy and young dog that you have been holding onto. Not only did you lose Pooh yesterday, but you lost the puppy Pooh, one year old Pooh, five year old Pooh. Get the picture?"

"I think so," I said.

"The sad piece is that your images of Pooh from yesterday kept you from being as present with her during these last few days as you could have been. When people identify with yesterday, they cannot see the present," Jesus added. "When you only could see Pooh for who she used to be, you distanced yourself from her aging."

"So memories are bad?" I asked.

"Lose the 'bad' evaluation," he said.

"Sorry," I said.

"Forget 'sorry.' Guilt won't serve you well here. Just see. Consider another example, like your inability to see your dog age, in a similar fashion, when an adult only sees a child as a child, in their mind, they can never see the adult." I quickly thought of my family. As the youngest of four children, one of my sisters still refers to me as "baby brother," a past image held tight. I also thought of children from past churches I served. I feel surprised every time I return to find how much they have grown. To see them as adults, I must release the image of them in my mind as children.

"Jesus," I said, "I'm still confused. If my pain over the death of my dog came from attachment, how can we love without being attached?" I asked.

"Perhaps the better question, how can you love when you are attached? Relationships overflowing with attachment and identification are so bound by images, memories, and expectations that very little seeing is done at all. All the relating exists between images, not people. Attachment also brings fear. Fear of losing the relationship, fear of something happening to the person, idea or thing you are attached to can dominate behavior. Afraid of loss, people tend to attempt controlling others to secure safety. The result is little authentic relating."

"Wow," I said. "I have so much to learn."

"You have so much to see," Jesus said. "For now, see your identifications. See your attachments," Jesus instructed.

We sat silently together. I let memories of family and pet cycle through. Jesus gave a sympathetic sigh. Then he was gone.

Movement:
From grasping which causes suffering
to letting go which brings peace.

Stepping Stone:
See your attachments.
Don't let them rule, no matter how painful.

Cayla, our oldest, went to Girl Scout camp at age six. Packing her bag with her the night before, rolling and rerolling her sleeping bag into as tiny a bundle as possible, Cayla was a little worried and teary about going to camp and spending three nights in a cabin away from home. As the good rational father, I assured her. "Here's what we know," I said, "lots of girls are going there every week and they come back okay. Your friend Coley went. She came back okay, and she had a good time."

The next day, we took her to camp. We left her stuff by a sign in the parking lot. We walked her into the cafeteria and through the registration line – no problems all her registration forms were in. We went through the nurse's line – no problems: no lice, no foot fungus. I was a proud papa. Then we sat at a table with another girl and one of her leaders. Cayla made her own name tag. I beamed, again a proud papa. I helped by introducing her to another camper sitting at the table. They smiled. Then a third girl came up. She was rude to her mother. I started to introduce Cayla to the third girl but decided that since she was so rude to her mother, I didn't care if Cayla met her or not.

As soon as they finished their nametags, they were going to go to their cabin where the other girls were – without us, without mom and dad, without we who loved her most. I thought to myself, 'What? I don't get to take her to her cabin? I don't get to set up her bunk? Why not? My parents always set up my bunk for me. I just have to leave her here in the cafeteria?' I realized that at some point I was going to have to leave so we hugged and kissed, said our goodbyes, and started toward the door. I looked back at Cayla, a mistake, for she was looking at me with her puppy dog eyes, those drooping you-are-leaving-me-here-in-a-cafeteria-with-this-girl-who-is-rude-to-her-mother-and-driving-away-just-like-that eyes.

We pulled out of the parking lot, Cayla's gaze still seared in my memory. Trying to be brave, but failing, I thought about the rude child at the table. I wondered who else Cayla would meet. Would they be nice to her?

"Forget this," I said, "let's go get her." Carrie tried to calm my fears, tried to help me be brave as a parent. That worked for a while as I rubbed my teary eyes on the way home.

The problem was, Cayla wasn't the only child I was thinking of, I thought of Thomas, a two year old little boy I heard about a few days before from friends of their family in our congregation. Thomas drowned. He had slipped away from his parents at a party and fell into a neighbor's pool. His parents loved him, cared for him, watched over him, yet, he still drowned. If Cayla was within my grasp, I felt I could protect her, but away from me, out of my reach, out of ear shot, I felt helpless.

I thought about leaving Cayla with people I didn't know. I thought about entrusting them with the life of my precious child. I wanted to take her home and go with her everywhere since I had heard about Thomas. About ten o'clock that night, I said to our church intern who was at our house, "Okay, I'm going to get her. You want to go with me?"

He replied, "She's probably already asleep."

"It's not about her, it's about me," I replied.

I started telling myself the same message I gave to Cayla. "Here's what we know, lots of girls are going there every week and they come back okay. Cayla's friend Coley went. She came back okay, and she had a good time." Cayla and I both survived her first trip to Girl Scout Camp though it wasn't easy for either of us.

Buddha said, "Life is suffering. Suffering comes from attachment."

The pain I felt came from the attachment I have to my daughter. I don't consider the pain 'bad.' I give thanks for that pain often. I feel pain for the people I care about. I see this pain as a part of my connection to them. Because I am attached to them, because they are important to me, I may experience pain at times, like when I dropped my daughter off for her overnight camp.

I also recognize that there is undue suffering from attachment: attachment that leads me to try and control all outer circumstances, attachment that encourages me to keep my children I care for under the false image that I can always protect them; attachment that wants the end of my pain through cowardly means; attachment that creates and recreates images as a substitute for reality. All these byproducts of attachment cause me to suffer needlessly and to impose suffering on others. Those attachments I can do without.

Where do you feel pain in your relationships? Is that pain something you celebrate or something you try to avoid?

Stepping Stone:
Let go of attachments to things.

Whereas my attachment to others may cause pain as a result of relating to others (After all, when approaching the grave of his dead friend Lazarus, Jesus wept (John 11:35)), attachment to things is unnecessary (see Jesus and the rich young man (Matthew 19:16f)). Grasping onto material things only causes unnecessary suffering.

I remember seeing a new BMW with bumper stickers all over the rear. There were so many bumper stickers I thought them more appropriate for the back of a Volkswagen Bus than a new BMW. Intrigued, I pulled closer. When I got close enough to read the first one, I could read no more for it made me laugh. The bumper sticker read, *The Best Things in Life Aren't Things.* I laughed because to me it seemed the person wanted to have it both ways, *The Best Things in Life Aren't Things - But Check Out My New BMW!*

Caring for people who are attached to things is problematic. Perhaps we should follow the example of this rabbi...

There once was an elderly man whose home burned down and in it were all that he possessed. The people in his town came out an offered sympathy. Late in the day, his rabbi arrived.

The rabbi put his hand on the man's shoulder in an embrace and said, "Well, this will make dying easier."

The lessons from Jesus, Buddha, and others who have overcome their attachments are similar to the rabbi's, not only does freeing ourselves from attachments make dying easier – freeing ourselves from attachments makes living easier, too.

What things in your life are you attached to? Are those attachments making your life better or weighing you down on your life's journey?

Stepping Stone:
Let go of attachments to the past.

I read of a woman who had been injured in an accident which affected her short term memory. She would meet the doctor, he would leave. When he returned, she would meet him again as if for the first time. On the fourth meeting, the doctor put a tack in his hand. When he shook her hand, she felt pain. He left. When he returned later, she did not recognize him but would not shake his hand. She remembered the previous pain somewhere in her mind and that shaped the pattern and expectation.

Past pain can shape our expectations and patterns. When my oldest daughter, Cayla, was about two years old, we were selling a car. The car was sitting in our driveway with a "For Sale" sign. About eight o'clock one night, someone drove by, saw the sign and decided to ask about the car. As the woman got out of her car and walked to our door, Pooh, our Labrador Retriever, then about three years old and with the eagerness and energy of a puppy but seventy pounds heavier, came around the side of the house to greet our guest. Unfortunately, the woman didn't speak non verbal dog and wrongly interpreted Pooh's hello as, "I'm going to eat you."

Inside, we heard the doorbell ring, then the screaming, the loud, continuous screaming, began.

I went to the door. I cautiously opened it. I saw the situation, opened the glass door and said, "Let her come in" meaning the dog. The screaming woman jumped in the house and even though the dog was now outside, the woman was still screaming. This terrified two year old Cayla.

For six weeks after that incident, every time the doorbell rang, Cayla screamed and ran to her mother. She was patterned by her pain. She still seems to show an aversion to used cars.

Our attachment to our past, whether trying to recreate pleasure or avoid pain, can keep us in a sleeping state unaware and unawake to the present moment. J. Krishnamurti wrote...

What is pleasure? How does it come about? You see a sunset, and seeing it gives you great delight. You experience it... and that experience leaves a memory of pleasure, and tomorrow you will want that pleasure repeated...this repetition takes place, as you can observe, when thought thinks about it and gives it vitality and continuity. It is the same with sex, the same with other forms of physical and psychological pleasure. Thought creates the image of that pleasure and keeps on thinking about it...

Stepping Stone:
*Let go of imaged yesterdays
to be present with each person you encounter.*

I spoke at a women's group lunch meeting for several churches in the county. During my talk, I noticed a woman down front smiling at me. I did not receive the smile well. "Why is she smiling?" I asked myself. "I don't care if she's smiling," I thought, "I don't like her."

What is amazing to me about preachers is, even during the middle of a speech, while we are talking, we can have internal conversations. "Why is she yawning? Am I boring? I hope not. Maybe she just stayed out late last night." What's even more amazing is that while we are giving a speech on the love of God, we can have an internal conversation about someone we don't like. I was having one of those about this woman. She was smiling, but I didn't like her. I didn't know why I didn't like her, I just didn't. After I finished speaking, during the luncheon, I saw her in line. I fell back and waited for her to get her food before I approached the buffet. After I got my food, I avoided where she was sitting. I wondered why I had such strong negative feelings about a person I had never met.

On my way home, I thought about this woman. I answered my own question. She reminded me of a woman in my first church who I thought questioned and disapproved of every idea I had. I had mentally placed a past frustration on this woman. A different person, but because she reminded me of some pain I had from my past, I avoided her and lost focus on my speech and my lunch.

Often, when we are with someone, we are anything but present. There is a Buddhist teaching that says we never experience the present moment, only the past. Because our minds are so full from all our images formed in our yesterdays, we have no todays. Instead of being with people we encounter, we bring past images which have little to do with the person and address those and only those.

What events from your past are shaping your life's present? Would your life be better if you let go of them?

Try this week to let go of the past and live in the present. When you are with someone, be with them. In each moment, be present.

Stepping Stone:
Let go of attachments and look for love.

J. Krishnamurti wrote on the distinction between love and attachment.

What is attachment? Why are we so attached to something or other – to property, money, to wife, to husband, to some foolish conclusion, to some ideological concept? Why are we so attached? Let us inquire into it together. And the consequences of attachment... if you observe it very closely, whether it be to a wife, husband, a boy or a girl, an idea, a picture, a memory, an experience, the consequences are that it breeds the fear of losing. And out of that fear there is jealously. How jealous we are. Jealous of those in power – you follow? All the jealousy. And from Jealousy there is hatred. Of course, jealousy is hatred. And when you are attached, there is always suspicion, secrecy. Haven't you noticed all this? It's so common in the world. And can you, if you are attached to something or some idea, some person, can you end it now? That is death. Which means, can you live with death all day long? Ah, think of it. Go into it. That is, not commit suicide, we are not talking of silly stuff, but to live with that, ending all sense of attachment, all having direction, purpose, all the rest of it. Acting. That is to live with death every second, never collecting, never gathering... That is real freedom. And from that freedom there is love. Love is not attachment.[8]

Attachment binds, but for love to exist, there must be freedom. Beyond attachment is liberation and from that liberation love becomes possible.

---

[8] J. Krishnamurti, *To Be Human*, p.156-157

The Enlightenment of Jesus:

Buddha said, "Life is suffering." The source of our suffering, according to Buddha, is attachment, clinging, grasping. Jesus also pointed out how attachment causes suffering, especially attachments to things.

Luke 12:[13] *Someone in the crowd said to (Jesus), "Teacher, tell my brother to divide the family inheritance with me."* [14] *But he said to him, "Friend, who set me to be a judge or arbitrator over you?"* [15] *And he said to them, "Take care! Be on your guard against all kinds of greed; for one's life does not consist in the abundance of possessions."* [16] *Then he told them a parable: "The land of a rich man produced abundantly.* [17] *And he thought to himself, 'What should I do, for I have no place to store my crops?'* [18] *Then he said, 'I will do this: I will pull down my barns and build larger ones, and there I will store all my grain and my goods.* [19] *And I will say to my soul, 'Soul, you have ample goods laid up for many years; relax, eat, drink, be merry.'* [20] *But God said to him, 'You fool! This very night your life is being demanded of you. And the things you have prepared, whose will they be?'* [21] *So it is with those who store up treasures for themselves but are not rich toward God."*

Jesus understood how temporary property can be, and how possessed we can get by our possessions. For Jesus, the only thing which carries beyond any moment is love, precisely because love and only love allows us to live in the moment.

Reflection:

Read the following quotes. How does each relate to the steps toward enlightenment described in this chapter?

Don't let yesterday use up too much of today.
Will Rogers

The past is already past.
Don't try to regain it.
The present does not stay.
Don't try to touch it.

From moment to moment.
The future has not come;
Don't think about it
Beforehand.
Layman P'ang

When mortals are alive, they worry about death.
When they're full, they worry about hunger.
Theirs is the Great Uncertainty.

But sages don't consider the past.
And they don't worry about the future.
Nor do they cling to the present.
And from moment to moment they follow the Way.
Bodhidharma

Just think of the trees: they let the birds perch and fly,
with no intention to call them when they come
and no longing for their return when they fly away.
If people's hearts can be like the trees,
they will not be off the Way.
Langya

Time is too slow for those who wait, too swift for those who fear, too long for
those who grieve, too short for those who rejoice; but for those who love, time
is eternity.
Henry Van Dyke

Now what?

On the tombstones on the following page, write the names of
people and objects you want to let go of, so that by letting go, you
might have more present relationships and live unattached to things.

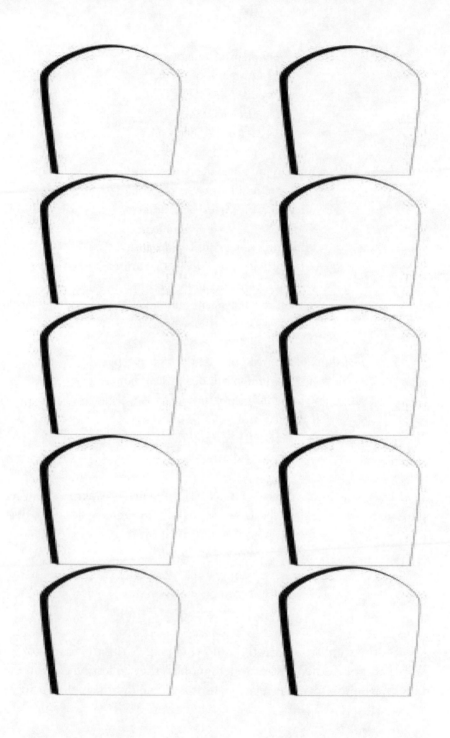

Encounter Nine:
Epilogue
Present Moment

You do not need to do anything;
you do not need to leave your room.
Remain sitting at your table and listen.
You do not even need to listen; just wait.
You do not even need to wait;
just become still, quiet and solitary
and the world will freely offer itself to you to be unmasked.
It has no choice. It will roll in ecstasy at your feet.
Franz Kafka

The next time I saw Jesus, we were in Michigan visiting Carrie's family. I had taken some time by myself, early in the morning, while others were still sleeping, to kayak on the Ausable River. Kayaking along, I saw few others on the river. I weaved between an occasional fly fisherman but mostly paddled alone.

Rounding a bend into a long straight stretch, I saw a man standing on the shore. As I got closer, and got a better look at him, I recognized Jesus. Amazingly, he walked across the water to my kayak. As he got closer, I realized that I was no longer moving though the river continued to flow around me.

"Enjoying your self?"

"Immensely," I said.

"I'm glad," Jesus said. "I enjoy seeing you at peace. There is seldom a time when you are more at peace then when you are in, on, or by water."

"True," I said still awing at the movement of the water and my stillness.

"This is you, now. You are like your kayak right now, though the water moves around your boat, the boat is still and calm. The boat is not reacting to the river, but able to act on its own. So it is with you in your life, though the world may move around you, you are still, calm, able to move independently."

I remembered the lake I had watched growing up. When the weather was calm, the surface of the lake was like glass. When a small wind blew, the lake was slightly rippled. When a large wind blew, there were big waves. When there was a storm, the lake was covered in white caps. I had been like the lake. Whatever the weather, I reacted. I wanted to be calm water no matter what was happening in the world around me. I wanted to be like my kayak right at that moment. Though the world might move around me, I wanted to be still.

Jesus continued, "Here, your spirit is calm. You are not resisting the river. You are not fighting the current. You are just beyond it, seeing it."

I noticed that my kayak was just a little above the water; the water barely touching the boat.

"I feel like my visits with you have led me to a great change in my life. I am more...awake."

"Yes, you are. You think less and observe more. You judge less and see more. You name and define less and you live more. You are more awake. No longer tossed about by every wind and wave, no longer carried along by every tide or current, you are more awake. You can see."

"I would like to see even more," I said. "I feel like I have snoozed through much of my life. How can I awaken to more of my life? I feel there are still so many times where I am not fully conscious. Right now, on the water, I feel like I am the person you described, but I am not like this much of the time."

"Yes," Jesus said, "but you are now. Do not worry about what you aren't at other times. Instead, appreciate the present moment, for right now, you are awake; right now, you are attentive; right now, you are aware. This is the moment that matters. Now."

The boat started to move in the flow of the river.

I smiled.

I ceased paddling and used my paddle as a rudder.

We floated along, together.

Jesus.

And I.